GOING DEEP IN PRAYER:

40 Days of In-Depth Prayer

Gil Stieglitz

Going Deep in Prayer – 40 Days of In-Depth Prayer

Published by: Principles to Live By, Roseville CA 95661
www.ptlb.com

All Scripture verses are from the New American Standard Bible
unless otherwise indicated. New American Standard Bible: 1995
update. 1995 La Habra, CA: The Lockman Foundation.

ISBN 978-0-9838602-9-7
Christian Living /Theology

Printed in the United State of America

Dedication

This book is dedicated to Jenessa Stieglitz, Abbey Stieglitz, and Grace Stieglitz, my three daughters who I have had the privilege of being their earthly father. It is my great delight that they have an active and personal relationship with their heavenly Father. I have lovingly spent many hours praying the contents of this book over each of them. They are some of the best treasure God has ever placed in my life. Because of them and their mother, I am a rich man indeed.

Table of Contents

Going Deep in Prayer - Part I

The Lord's Prayer

The Fruit of the Spirit

Various Forms of Prayer

The Ten Major Relationships of Life

Going Deep in Prayer - Part II

Introduction

One of the greatest things that Christians can do is talk to their heavenly Father. It brings answers, it gives peace, it deepens the dialogue between God and ourselves, and it changes us. And yet most Christians will confess that they do not pray as much as they should. Why don't we pray as much as we think we should? I am convinced that it is because people don't know what to pray. The average Christian if asked to pray privately or publically will be completely out of things to say to God in five minutes. They know how to pray, but they don't know what to pray. Therefore they allow their prayer life to dwindle to those times of crisis and/ or pain when there is nothing else to do but plead what we need with overpowering emotions.

This book celebrates praying by giving the average Christian great stuff to talk with God about. It is not a clever book on motivation or how prayer works; it is just simple suggestions for forty days of things to pray about with God and watch Him work. I believe the more we communicate with God and pray for what we know He wants, the more we understand His heart and then the more accurate our prayers will be in asking for His will for our lives. We also will see more answers to prayer when we pray biblical ideas instead of selfish desires.

You will find some of the topics will fascinate you and encourage long conversations with God. Other topics will leave you flat when you try and pray them; pray them anyway. Keep talking with God about these various issues, and you will finally be satisfied with your prayer life and you will be much closer to God.

Prayer is simply talking with God. It is asking, talking, crying, screaming, listening, arguing, and all kinds of other things that make for a dynamic relationship. I am convinced that most people do not pray more because they run out of things to pray. If we talked with God more and saw answers to our questions, answers to our requests, and progress in our spiritual lives then we would be drawn into a deeper and richer prayer life. This book is designed to make that process happen.

This book is designed to encourage you to pray more about a broader range of topics than you would normally pray. Therefore this book is arranged alphabetically with prayer topics that start with A and B and C and so on. Each topic has suggested things to talk with God about in relation to that topic. I fully expect that some of the topics will trigger long discussions with God and others will just be short sentence prayers. It is all okay. Just begin talking with God about all of life and things will change.

Why do we have to pray?

Why do we need to pray, work, and do the thousand other things that are required to get by in this world if there is an omnipotent God?

Realize that God purposely creates unfinished projects that we as humans must complete. He seems to do this so that we get involved and have ownership in our life and our world. God could clearly make everything complete and perfect, so that we do not have to do anything. But He has chosen, through His infinite wisdom, to leave many things unfinished. He wants us involved in the outworking of the completed project. Look at the nature of the world that God has created. Some things are complete and many things about our individual human lives are incomplete.

Our whole life is an unfinished project that can go in a lot of different ways. He has not predetermined everything we will do with our life (even though He does know). Our life is an opportunity that He gives us to choose to use the talents, skills, relationships, and situations that come our way to build a life that blesses Him and gives us satisfaction. Those people who moan and whine that life is not fair because someone else has less difficulties or more money at the start of life, often do not realize that life is an unfinished project that God wants you to build out with Him guiding the decisions that you make. If you just wait for God or someone else to give you finished opportunities to enjoy, inhabit, or consume, your life will be miserable. It is in the building, designing, creating, testing, and working that life is lived. This is true of every part of life. This is the way that God made the life of humans.

The nature of relationships is that they are unfinished projects and must be completed by our communication, service, care, patience, and the like. God could have made us so that we did not need to communicate through external speech, but He did not because He wanted us to have to complete the relationship through our speaking with another person. It is required. We cannot read each other's thoughts. We must talk to another person to have a relationship.

Children are another unfinished project that God planned into our world. He could have started the world with every person who will eventually inhabit heaven, but He chose to have people born in a long time sequence at least 10,000 years. And He chose to have people start completely dependent and grow up through an 18-to-25 year process requiring other adult involvement. Other species God created have litters and the parents walk away within weeks of the birth to never see the children again. He specifically designed child rearing as an unfinished project which will take years of investment on the parent's part. This is a tremendous amount of work, but raising children well brings a satisfaction that is very hard to put into words.

The need for prayer is an unfinished project that God has purposely put into our universe. God could have made the world any way that He wanted. He could have had the things that we needed just show up at the exact time and place that they were going to be needed, but He did not. He decided that some things will show up without our involvement, but many things will not show up unless we pray. There are many things that God will do without prayer, but there are many things in each of our individual lives that He will not do unless we pray. Our prayer is an essential element in completing our highest potential.

Even God's answers to our prayer are often unfinished projects. He wants us to learn something, develop something, invest in something, and sense something by completing the project. Remember that He can do anything He wants and yet He still sends unfinished projects that have "some assembly required." This is for our benefit not His. We gain and grow and become something by throwing ourselves into the projects that He obviously wants us to be a part of. If He did not then we would be like the boy who sought to help the butterfly out of the chrysalis. He cut the cocoon open and released the butterfly only to discover that the butterfly needed to push against the sides of the cocoon to force blood into its wings and strengthen the muscles of the wing. Because He eliminated the struggle, the butterfly had useless wings and soon died. God knows what we need more than we do, and He sends these work projects and opportunities for us to become all that He planned for us.

In the garden of Eden before the fall of mankind into sin, the life that God gave Adam and Eve was full of unfinished projects. They had to tend and keep the garden, name the animals, eat, sleep, etc. Therefore God's infinite wisdom designs unfinished projects for us so that our lives will have meaning, purpose, and satisfaction. When sin entered the picture and man became a selfish, rebellious creature, the unfinished assignments of God did not stop. They are now interrupted by the imperfect and selfish actions of humanity and angels.

How to Use This Book

There are a number of different ways of praying detailed in this book. You might start by committing to pray five minutes each day for forty days, taking a different section each day. Some days you may pray for more than five minutes but other days just the five minutes. Each day will take between five minutes and thirty minutes to pray. These prayer exercises are not meant to be a burden but to introduce you to the wonder of praising God. Each section in this book has more than enough material to last for five minutes.

Because there is more than enough material to praise God for five minutes, this book can be repeated over and over again praying the material that was not prayed the first time through. When a praise exercise asks you to write down things that you can praise God about, go ahead and write those things in the book. It will be tremendously encouraging the next time you go through the book to see those and to write down new ones you did not remember the last time through the book.

Some have even added these exercises as a regular part of their devotional time, repeatedly going through these praise exercises as a small part of their larger devotional time with the Lord.

Some have designated a particular day of the week that they will do these praise exercises and doing other prayer exercises on other days. This turns this book into forty weeks of praise.

You might pray one of these sections per day for forty days. This will take longer than five minutes each day, but it increases the spiritual adventure.

You might pray one of these sections for five minutes at the top of each hour during the typical work day. You might pray one of these sections for five-ten minutes at 6 a.m.; 9 a.m.; 12 noon; 3 p.m.; 6 p.m.; 9 p.m.

Whichever level of involvement you choose, you will see an increase in your prayer life. You will see an increase in the answers and in the changes in your life and others. Don't miss this opportunity to connect to what God wants to do in your world through prayer.

Some churches have used this book for their small groups studies. Usually small groups use this material in two ways. One way is as a part of their small group time together, setting aside five to ten minutes to praise God using these praise exercises each time the group meets. This is a way to worship without singing and to learn about God in every group. A second way to use the material for small groups is to use these praise exercises as the focus of the group. This is where the whole group meets to praise God using one or a number of the praise exercises. These praise sessions will last thirty minutes to an hour with everyone having pushed into the presence of God and been touched by Him.

Some churches use these praise exercises as a way to teach the doctrine of God. There are few things as dynamic as learning who God is by praising Him for each aspect of who He has revealed Himself to be.

Some churches even use this type of praise exercise as a way of praying for the worship services before and during the service itself. This is a powerful way of drawing God's presence and power to the large public services of the church.

Going Deep in Prayer - Part I

Day 1: Our Father who art in heaven

The Lord's Prayer for His Disciples

The Lord's Prayer is really Jesus' training for his disciples on how to pray to the Father. Each of the requests in the prayer is a topic to spend time talking with God about. This prayer was not meant to just be a mantra that is repeated over and over again.

* Pray the topics of the Lord's Prayer that Jesus instructs us to spend time on. Ask God for ten things under each topic that would be in line with His will.

Our Father who art in Heaven hallowed be Thy Name
* Hallow His name by lifting it up in praise.
* Give thanks to God for who He is and what He has done for you.

Omnipresent: Everywhere present; **Omniscient:** All-knowing and All-wise; **Omnipotent:** All-powerful; **Immutable:** Unchanging; **Holy:** Transcendent, Pure, Righteous; **Good:** Loving, Merciful, Gracious, Long-suffering; **True:** Undeceptive, Faithful; **Sovereign:** In charge and in control.

* What can you do or say today that would remind you how holy and majestic God is?
* What has God done in your life for which you can praise His name and in that way honor and glorify Him?

Day 2: Thy Kingdom come

Thy Kingdom come

- Ask God that He would bring His kingdom to earth both through his servants in the present age and actually coming to rule and reign on the earth as King of the Earth.

What are the most exciting aspects of Jesus bringing His kingdom to this earth today?

- Pray about those things beginning to happen soon.

If Christ's kingdom were to begin today, what would be different?

- Ask God to begin doing those things.
  1.
  2.
  3.
  4.
  5.
  6.
  7.
  8.
  9.
  10.

- Ask God to bring His kingdom through you to the people that you meet today; that they would see what God would do in your world.

What aspects of the kingdom can you ask God to bring through you today?

- Justice, love, mercy, righteousness, healing, hope

Day 3: Thy will be done

Thy will be done on earth as it is in heaven
- Ask God to change the specific things you see happening that are clearly not His will.

What ten aspects of your community are clearly not the way God would want things to be?
- Pray about those things changing.
- Ask God to show you how to be involved today, this week, and this month in bringing an aspect of the kingdom to this world.

Thy will be done on earth as it is in heaven.
1.
2.
3.
4.
5.
6.
7.
8.
9.
10.

Day 4: Give us this day

Give us this day our daily bread

Pray for your relational, physical, emotional, spiritual, mental, financial, and vocational needs to be met.

- Relational

- Physical

- Emotional

- Spiritual

- Mental

- Financial

- Vocational

- What ten things do you need in order to be the best possible you? Ask Him specifically to do those things for you.

Give us this day our daily bread.
1.
2.
3.
4.
5.
6.
7.
8.
9.
10.

Day 5: Forgive us our trespasses

And forgive us our trespasses as we forgive those who trespass against us

- Ask God to forgive you for your sins as you, by an act of your will, choose to forgive those who have wronged you.
- Who do you need to forgive – forgive them in prayer.
- What do you need to forgive others for – forgive them in prayer.
- What do you need to forgive yourself for – let it go in prayer.

Forgive us our trespasses as we forgive those who trespass against us.

1.
2.
3.
4.
5.
6.
7.
8.
9.
10.

Day 6: Lead us not into temptation

And lead us not into temptation but deliver us from evil

* Ask God to point out when you are facing temptation and to clearly show you the way away from it and toward something righteous.

Pride

Envy

Anger

Lust

Sloth

Gluttony

Greed

What ten different ways are temptation and evil seeking to get you off the righteous path?

* Ask God to protect you from each of these.

1.
2.
3.
4.
5.
6.
7.
8.
9.
10.

* Ask God to show you what you must do to protect yourself.

Day 7: For Thine is the kingdom and the glory

For Thine is the kingdom and the glory and the power forever. Amen

* Pray for eyes to see what God is doing.

What ten things is God doing in your region?
1.
2.
3.
4.
5.
6.
7.
8.
9.
10.

Ask God to show you how to be a part of His kingdom solution.
1.
2.
3.
4.
5.
6.
7.
8.
9.
10.

Day 8: Love

Praying through the fruit of the Spirit

In Galatians 5:22, 23, we are given the fruit of the Spirit which are Love, Joy, Peace, Patience, Kindness, Goodness, Meekness, Faithfulness, and Self-Control. One of the goals of being a Christian is to have the qualities of the fruit of the Spirit flowing from your life constantly. This prayer exercise is designed to get you to ask God more specifically to make that a reality in your life.

Love: To love means to meet needs, to pursue, to please

- Pray that God would show you those with a need that you can meet.
- Pray that you will realize when love means pursuing someone's soul.
- Pray that you will be alert to how to righteously please others.
- Pray that you are sensitive to the Holy Spirit's promptings to meet someone's need, pursue their soul, or please them.
- Pray that God would give you the wisdom and insight into when love has to be tough, negative, and discerning.
- Pray that you would allow God to flow through you to others who you may not want to love.
- Ask God to show you if the people in your life feel overwhelmed by the amount or quality of your love for them.
- Pray that God would show you how to righteously love Him.
- Pray that God would show you how to biblically love yourself.

- Pray that God would show you how to love your spouse
- Pray that God would show you how to love your family.
- Pray that God would show you how to love your friends in new ways.
- Pray that God would allow you to love your colleagues, bosses, and subordinates in a deeper more Christian way.
- Pray that God would allow you to love your community in a powerful way to bring glory to God.
- Pray that God allows you to love your enemies.

Day 9: Joy

Joy: God's positive outlook and deepening relationships

- Pray that God increases your joy.
- Pray that God strengthens you to make new mental choices.
- Ask God to fill your mind with positive pictures. Philippians 4:8
- Ask God to repair damaging memories of the past with understanding about the good that came from it.
- Ask God to give you the ability to make new emotional choices. Ephesians 4:32
- Ask God to develop a gladness in serving Him. Philippians 2:1-3
- Ask God to show you where and how you can express gratefulness. Ephesians 4:29
- Ask God to show you how to wrap the truth in love. Ephesians 4:15
- Ask God to give you a generous heart. 1 Timothy 6:9,10

Day 10: Peace

Peace: Stop needless fighting and live in harmony with others

- Ask God to develop harmony with His plan, others, and yourself.
- Ask God to give you the courage to say you were wrong.
- Ask God to show you the second-mile project that will erase bitterness in your heart towards another person.
- Ask God to help you see the common enemy that is really causing the trouble between you and a loved one.
- Ask God to give you energy to work hard even where there is no peace.
- Ask God that He remind you regularly to keep short accounts with Him.
- Ask God to set your mind on the things of the Spirit so that you will experience life and peace.
- Ask God to empower you to replace selfish and sinful thoughts with righteous ones.
- Ask God to show you when the Adversary is behind your lack of peace: Ephesians 6:12; Matthew 4:3-11; Matthew 16:21-23
- Ask God to empower you to rebuke or educate the intermediate cause of your lack of peace: Matthew 16:21-23; Proverbs 15:1; 17:10: Luke 17:3
- Ask God to strengthen you to resist the intent of the Devil in your lack of peace. James 4:7

Day 11: Patience

Patience: Giving God and others time and space to act

- Ask God to show you the size and fullness of the box that He has you in.
- Ask God to make you understand that He wants you to stay in His box without cheating your way out.
- Ask God to keep you from becoming despondent or depressed when the box doesn't open or expand.
- Ask God to keep you energized with the tasks you are to complete in the box.
- Ask God to remind you to allow Him the time He wants or needs to open or expand the box.
- Ask God to show you all the adjustments to the box you can make.
- Ask God to show you clearly why the box is the size it is and how to endure its size.
- Ask God to cause you to keep pushing forward and seeing if the box will expand or open -- not give up.
- Ask God to deflect and strengthen you to resist temptation in the midst of the sameness.

Day 12: Kindness

Kindness: Pleasant helpfulness

- Ask God to muzzle your cynical tongue.
- Ask God to clearly give you kind, edifying words.
- Ask God to show you the positive achievement that is possible in the other person.
- Pray that God will fill you with His love and pleasant helpfulness for others.
- Pray that God would show you needs that you can meet.
- Ask God to give you a new ability to hold back doing any evil that you could do.
- Ask God to fill your mind with the encouraging word.
- Ask God to develop in you a listening ear.
- Ask God to give you the ability to let grudges go and fully forgive. 2 Timothy 2:24
- Ask God to give you a pleasantness in the midst of the drudgery of life. Titus 2:5

Day 13: Goodness

Goodness: Providing true benefit to another

- Ask God to show you the beneficial acts that you should begin doing.
- Ask God to keep you from doing or even seeing the beneficial acts that would deter you from your goals.
- Ask God to fill your mouth with beneficial things to say.
- Ask God to give you the boldness to really help people and not just make nice.
- Ask God to make you constantly aware of the difference between justice, mercy, and goodness.
- Ask God to show you how to share goodness down the priority structure.

Day 14: Meekness

Meekness: Being flexible, calm, and adaptable

- Ask God for a new level of flexibility.
- Ask God for the ability to delay your desires from becoming expectations.
- Ask God for the impulse to make thoughtful requests instead of angry demands.
- Ask God to give you a calm adaptability when things don't go the way you would like.
- Ask God to clearly show you the size of the box or lot that you live in.
- Ask God to give you a new level of graciousness when the box changes size.
- Ask God to give you a new ability to deny yourself for the good of others and the kingdom.
- Tell God that you are okay with His control of the size of your box.
- Ask God to show you the areas where you have not surrendered control of your box to Him.

Day 15: Faithfulness

Faithfulness: Persevering and enduring

- Pray that God would show you what results staying faithful will have in your life.
- Pray that God will let you see the reasons why you should stay faithful.
- Ask God to give you a new level of joy in the midst of enduring faithfulness.
- Pray that God forgives your lack of faithfulness in the past.
- Thank Him for the forgiveness that is Jesus Christ's death for you.
- Pray that your faithfulness in the area that you don't want to be will be a testimony to the existence of God, the truth of a moral life, and your place in heaven.
- Pray that you would not be faithful to the wrong things and thereby waste your life.
- Ask for wisdom as to who needs your faithfulness today.
- Offer your faithfulness for one more day as a gift to God.
- Pray that God will give you a firm grasp of the heavenly and earthly rewards waiting for those who remain faithful to righteous relationships.

Day 16: Self-Control

Self-control: Moderation in all things

- Pray that God would show you where you are living outside of God's righteous boundaries of moderation.
- Ask God to show you who is being affected by your excess.
- Pray that you will find a new ability to moderate your desires and say no to excess today.
- Pray that you will be instant in your obedience to the prompting of the Spirit when He prompts you to do something other than involving yourself with the object of your excess.
- Pray that your heart would let go of the treasured place the excess has in your life.
- Ask God for new power to say no long before you are faced with the power of the temptation.
- Ask God for a vision of your life if you conquer your areas of excess.
- Ask God for a vision of your life if you do not conquer your areas of excess.

Day 17: Adoration of God

Various Forms of Prayer

The Scriptures list many types of prayers that a believer should offer up to God. These prayers represent a wide range of interactions with God. This next section covers some of these different types of prayer.

Adoration of God

1 Timothy 6:13-17

I charge you in the presence of God, who gives life to all things, and of Christ Jesus, who testified the good confession before Pontius Pilate, that you keep the commandment without stain or reproach until the appearing of our Lord Jesus Christ, which He will bring about at the proper time—He who is the blessed and only Sovereign, the King of kings and Lord of lords, who alone possesses immortality and dwells in unapproachable light, whom no man has seen or can see. To Him be honor and eternal dominion! Amen. Instruct those who are rich in this present world not to be conceited or to fix their hope on the uncertainty of riches, but on God, who richly supplies us with all things to enjoy.

Adore, glorify, honor, and magnify God for who He is. He describes Himself in the Bible in terms of five aspects of His being:

His Essence
    Infinite Genesis 21:33
    Self-Existent Acts 17:24, 25
    Spirit John 4:24

His Attributes
Omniscient Matthew 11:21
Omnipotent Job 9:4
Omnipresent Psalm 139 7-12
Immutable Psalms 102:25-27
Holiness 1 Peter 1:14-16
Righteous/Just Deuteronomy 32:4
Goodness Exodus 33:19
Long-suffering Genesis 6:3
Truth Isaiah 44:8, 9
Sovereign Exodus 34:6, 7

Exodus 34:5-8
Then the LORD passed by in front of him and proclaimed, "The LORD, the LORD God, compassionate and gracious, slow to anger, and abounding in lovingkindness and truth; who keeps lovingkindness for thousands, who forgives iniquity, transgression and sin..." Moses made haste to bow low toward the earth and worship.

His Nature
Tri-une: Father; Son, and Holy Spirit   Matthew 28:18-20

His Names
El: The Mighty God   Genesis 7:1
Elohim: The Creator – Powerful God   Genesis 1:1
El Shaddai: The Lord of Host   Genesis 17:1, 2
Adonai: Lord   2 Samuel 7:18-20
Yahweh: I AM   Genesis 2
Jehovah Jireh: The Lord who provides   Genesis 22:14

His Works

> **Creation**:   Genesis 1:1; Psalm 19:1
> **Exodus**:   1 Corinthians 10:1
> **Salvation**:   Ephesians 3:17
> **Scriptures**:   2 Timothy 3:16

- Spend time magnifying God and adoring Him for who He describes Himself to be.

If you would like to go more in depth in the adoration of God, check out the author's book, *Touching the Face of God: 40 Days of Adoring God.*

Romans 11:33-36

> *Oh, the depth of the riches both of the wisdom and knowledge of God! How unsearchable are His judgments and unfathomable His ways... For from Him and through Him and to Him are all things. To Him be the glory forever. Amen.*

Day 18: Biblical Prayer

Praying the prayers recorded in the Scriptures puts you in tune
with the Spirit of God.   Read and then pray the following biblical
prayers. Choose one or two to pray through slowly.

* **1 Chronicles 4:9**
  *Now Jabez called on the God of Israel, saying, " Oh that
  Thou wouldst bless me indeed, and enlarge my border, and
  that Thy hand might be with me, and that Thou wouldst
  keep me from harm, that it may not pain me!" And God
  granted him what he requested.*

* **Psalm 119:33**
  *Teach me, O Lord the way of Thy Statutes and I shall
  observe it to the end. Give me understanding, that I may
  observe Thy Law. And keep it with all my heart. Make me
  walk in the path of Thy commandments. For I delight in it.
  Incline my heart to Thy testimonies and not to dishonest
  gain.*

* **Romans 8: 26**
  *And in the same way the Spirit also helps our weakness;
  for we do not know how to pray as we should, but the
  Spirit Himself intercedes for us with groanings too deep
  for words.*

* **2 Corinthians 13: 7**
  *Now we pray to God that you do no wrong; not that we
  ourselves may appear approved, but that you may do what
  is right, even though we should appear unapproved.*

* **2 Corinthians 13:9**
  *For we rejoice when we ourselves are weak but you are
  strong; this we also pray for, that you be made complete.*

* **Ephesians 1:18-19**
  *I pray that the eyes of your heart may be enlightened, so
  that you may know what is the hope of His calling, what*

39

are the riches of the glory of His inheritance in the saints, and what is the surpassing greatness of His power toward us who believe.

- **Philippians 1: 9-11**
And this I pray, that your love may abound still more and more in real knowledge and all discernment, so that you may approve the things that are excellent, in order to be sincere and blameless until the day of Christ; having been filled with the fruit of righteousness which comes through Jesus Christ, to the glory and praise of God.

- **Colossians 1:9-12**
For this reason also, since the day we heard of it, we have not ceased to pray for you and to ask that you may be filled with the knowledge of His will in all spiritual wisdom and understanding, so that you may walk in a manner worthy of the Lord, to please Him in all respects, bearing fruit in every good work and increasing in the knowledge of God; strengthened with all power, according to His glorious might, for the attaining of all steadfastness and patience; joyously giving thanks to the Father, who has qualified us to share in the inheritance of the saints in light.

- **1 Thessalonians 5:16-22**
Rejoice always; pray without ceasing; in everything give thanks; for this is God's will for you in Christ Jesus. Do not quench the Spirit; do not despise prophetic utterances. But examine everything carefully; hold fast to that which is good; abstain from every form of evil.

- **2 Thessalonians 2:11**
To this end also we pray for you always that our God may count you worthy of your calling, and fulfill every desire for goodness and the work of faith with power;

- **2 Thessalonians 3:5**
  ... may the Lord direct your hearts into the love of God and into the steadfastness of Christ
- **2 Timothy 1:8**
  Therefore I want the men in every place to pray, lifting up holy hands, without wrath and dissension.
- **Philemon 4-6**
  I thank my God always, making mention of you in my prayers, because I hear of your love, and of the faith which you have toward the Lord Jesus, and toward all the saints; and I pray that the fellowship of your faith may become effective through the knowledge of every good thing which is in you for Christ's sake.
- **James 5: 13-14,16**
  Is anyone among you suffering? Let him pray. Is anyone cheerful? Let him sing praises. Is anyone among you sick?... Therefore, confess your sins to one another, and pray for one another, so that you may be healed. The effective prayer of a righteous man can accomplish much.
- **3 John 2**
  Beloved, I pray that in all respects you may prosper and be in good health, just as your soul prospers.

Day 19: Confession of Sin

Confession means to agree with God and His position about something you did, said, or thought about doing. It is often negative, but it can be positive.

Pride
- Confess any times you were arrogant, haughty, proud, or prejudiced in the last week.

Envy
- Confess any times you were envious in the last week.

Anger
- Confess any times you were angry in the last week.

Lust
- Confess any times you were lustful in the last week.

Sloth
- Confess any times you were slothful, procrastinating, or halfhearted in the last week.

Gluttony
- Confess any times that you stuffed yourself with food or drink well past moderation.

Greed
- Confess any times when you strove after money, possessions, or things more than God.

Day 20: The Armor of God

One of the crucial things that Christians must realize is that they are in a spiritual battle every day of their lives. God says to protect ourselves, we need the armor of God. One of the key ways that we put on the armor of God is through prayer.

Ephesians 6: 10-18

Finally, be strong in the Lord, and in the strength of His might. Put on the full armor of God, that you may be able to stand firm against the schemes of the devil. For our struggle is not against flesh and blood, but against the rulers, against the powers, against the world forces of this darkness, against the spiritual forces of wickedness in the heavenly places. Therefore, take up the full armor of God, that you may be able to resist in the evil day, and having done everything, to stand firm. Stand firm therefore, HAVING GIRDED YOUR LOINS WITH TRUTH, and HAVING PUT ON THE BREASTPLATE OF RIGHTEOUSNESS, and having shod YOUR FEET WITH THE PREPARATION OF THE GOSPEL OF PEACE; in addition to all, taking up the shield of faith with which you will be able to extinguish all the flaming missiles of the evil one. And take THE HELMET OF SALVATION, and the sword of the Spirit, which is the word of God. With all prayer and petition pray at all times in the Spirit, and with this in view, be on the alert with all perseverance and petition for all the saints, and pray on my behalf, that utterance may be given to me in the opening of my mouth, to make known with boldness the mystery of the gospel...

Truth; Righteousness; Peace; Faith; Salvation; Word of God; Prayer

Truth
- Ask God to remind you of the foundational Christian truths: God, Jesus, Holy Spirit, Man, Sin, Salvation, Church, Angels, Afterlife, Return of Christ.
- Ask God to show you the way that Satan is scheming to damage you; distorting the truth in your life.

Righteousness
- Ask God to cover you again in all the righteousness that is in Christ.
- Ask God to cause you to see what righteousness in your particular circumstance is and how you can participate with it.
- Ask God to empower you to live righteously today.

Peace
- Ask God to cover you with the peace that is only in the Lord Jesus Christ.
- Ask God to show you how the Devil is trying to rob you of peace.
- Ask God to show you how you can be the maker of peace.

Faith
- Ask God to strengthen your trust in Him rather than going after the temporary gain of sin and evil.
- Ask God to strengthen your grasp of the Christian Faith: The Ten Cardinal Christian Doctrines: God; Jesus; Holy Spirit; Mankind; Sin; Salvation; Angels; Church; Afterlife: Heaven, Hell, Judgment day; Return of Christ.
- Ask God to show you how you are not trusting Him.

Salvation

- Ask God to increase your grasp on the facts of your salvation
- Ask God to show you how Satan is distorting the truth about salvation
- Ask God to develop a new joy in your salvation

Word of God

- Ask God to arm you with just the right verses that will allow you to defeat the Devil's attacks that day.
- Ask God to make you alert to the promptings of the Holy Spirit.
- Ask God to cause you to apply the verses that He puts on your mind.
- Ask God to show you how the Devil is distorting the Scripture in your life.

Prayer

- Pray that God protects you, your family, your ministry, the church facilities, friends, and those who are under demonic attack.
- Pray that God gives you insight into what needs to be done to win.
- Pray in the name of the Lord Jesus Christ to bind the forces of darkness so that they would not be able to accomplish their goals.
- Pray that God would show you the ways the enemy is afflicting you.

Day 21: Entreaty

Entreaty is a form of prayer in which believers ask God to bless them. Ask God to bless you as Jabez did. This is what entreaty is all about -- bless me God in these ways:

- In our relationship with Him
- In our relationship with ourselves
- In our relationship with our spouse
- In our relationships with our family
- In our relationships at work
- In our relationships at church
- In our country
- In our finances
- In our friendships

- Ask Him for greater intimacy, discipline, knowledge, and respect.
- Ask Him what you can to do increase the sense of His presence in your life.

Day 22: Giving Thanks

Give thanks to God for everything that is happening in your life:

- At work
- With friends
- With your finances
- With your church
- With your health
- With your marriage or romantic life
- With your family
- With community, city, region, or state
- Especially for the hard things

What could God be trying to teach you?

What could God be trying to accomplish through you?

Day 23: Friendship with God

God asked us to come to Him as our High Priest. He can sympathize with our weakness. Tell God everything you are feeling and thinking as you would a close friend or a counselor. Lord, honestly I think this... Lord, I feel...

Tell Him about
- Your feelings
- Your thoughts
- Your goals
- Your obstacles
- Your fears
- Your love life
- Your family
- Your work
- Your sins
- Your struggles
- Your anger
- Your enemies

Day 24: Intercession

Ask God for what you should pray for the following people or activities and then ask Him for those things that He puts on your mind:

- Spouse
- Children
- Relatives
- Friends
- Ministry
- Other Christians
- Christian leaders
- People at work
- Neighbors
- People in the community
- People in leadership
- Business people

Day 25: Listening

Sit in a quiet place able to hear what God might be prompting you. Sit with an open Bible ready to turn and read God's Word and its application to your situation.

Listen to what God is saying about:

- Your life
- Your relationship with God
- Your personal development
- Your marriage
- Your family
- Your work
- Your church
- Your finances
- Your enemies

Day 26: Anxiety, Worry, Concerns

Philippians 4:6,7

> *Be anxious for nothing, but in everything by prayer and supplication with thanksgiving let your requests be made known to God. And the peace of God, which surpasses all comprehension, will guard your hearts and your minds in Christ Jesus.*

God tells us to bring our worries, anxieties, and concerns to Him rather than let them trouble our minds. This means that we should tell God what we are worried about and even what we think is the fix for it. Make a very specific request about what you would like God to do to deal with your anxiety, worry, or concern. It is not guaranteed that God will answer your request, but you will have His peace as you live out His answer.

- What are you anxious, worried, or concerned about?

- What would you like to see happen instead of all the things that your mind can imagine happening?

- Do all the righteousness you know and leave it in His hands.

Day 27: Ten Commandments

One of the consistent prayer guides down through the centuries of Christianity is to use the Ten Commandments. Each commandment is a topic as well as prohibition. Pray about the various ideas, actions, sub-topics, and even personal items that fall under that topic. Martin Luther, who started the Protestant Reformation, prayed through the Ten Commandments many times every day.

Thou shall have no other gods before me Thou
shall not make for yourself any graven images
Thou shall not take the name of the Lord thy God in vain
Remember the Sabbath Day to keep it holy
Honor your Father and your Mother
Thou shall not murder
Thou shall not commit adultery
Thou shall not steal
Thou shall not bear false witness against thy neighbor
Thou shall not covet any thing that belongs to your neighbor

- Pray that you would stay well inside of the boundaries of the Ten Commandments.
- Pray that you would erect effective barriers to keep you from violating any of the Ten Commandments.
- Pray that you would do the positive in the other direction of the commandment.
- Pray that God would clearly show your country, community, and region that there are consequences to violating God's moral law.
- Pray that God would show you how to be a part of the promotion of righteousness through either preventing violation of the commandment; seeking social justice because of its violation; or helping recovery from the

effects of themselves or others violating one of the commandments

- Pray that it would be clear why, where, and how the Ten Commandments moral standards need to be applied to a society.

1 Timothy 1:8-11

But we know that the Law is good, if one uses it lawfully, realizing the fact that law is not made for a righteous man, but for those who are lawless and rebellious, for the ungodly and sinners, for the unholy and profane, for those who kill their fathers or mothers, for murderers and immoral men and homosexuals and kidnappers and liars and perjurers, and whatever else is contrary to sound teaching

- Pray that God would cause the society to see the moral boundaries of the Ten Commandments and the benefits of living in them.
- Pray that God would be exalted in the society, not just in the church.
- Pray that God would clear up misrepresentations of Himself in society.
- Ask that God would increase the level of civility, kindness, and encouragement in the world – beginning with you.
- Ask God to remind the general society that they need to rest, worship, and center their lives on God not pleasure, power, or money.
- Pray that God will cause people to realize how important the family is as the bedrock of society.
- Pray that the society would recognize and exalt the incredible value of ordinary mothers and fathers in some new ways.

- Ask God to reinforce in humanity how vital it is to value human life.
- Pray that God shows the society that devaluing individual humans in any way damages the society as a whole: racism, abortion, elder abuse, sexism, etc.
- Pray that the society becomes willing to punish those who murder and that others will not follow their example.
- Ask God to quickly humble those who seek power through violence and/or the threat of violence.
- Pray that God would assist and highly bless those who are sexually faithful.
- Pray that our society would recognize the huge damage that comes from sexual infidelity.
- Ask God that our eyes would be opened to all the ways that our culture promotes stealing.
- Pray that individuals would wake up and stop stealing from each other, from work, from government, from their children, and from themselves.
- Pray that God would expose all the get-rich-quick schemes and scams that are forms of stealing.
- Ask God to close your mouth when you are about to lie.
- Ask God to build an honest society where people keep their word.
- Pray that people would change their ways of getting out of things they said they would do if it isn't written down.
- Ask God to build hope in our society that the blessings of others can be your blessings through hard work, team work, creativity, and fair play.
- Ask God to overturn the schemes of people to defraud people of their goods.

- Ask God to cause people to stop mentally scheming about having the specific blessings of another: their car, their house, their employees, their spouse, their technology.
- Pray that God shows us that there is always another way and a better way than to scheme after someone else's blessings.

Day 28: Beatitudes

The Beatitudes are the opening to the greatest sermon ever preached and detail the basic character of Christ. True believers have memorized and prayed the Beatitudes since Jesus uttered them.

Blessed are the poor in spirit for theirs is the kingdom of heaven
- Pray that God will develop a new level of humility in your life.
- Pray that you become more teachable.
- Pray that you develop the focus of looking to make others successful.
- Pray that God gives you a new ability to submit to those over you in joy.

Blessed are those who mourn for they shall be comforted
- Pray that God would develop a new level of brokenness in your life.
- Pray for brokenness over your sins.
- Pray for new awareness of personal responsibility in life.
- Pray for a willingness to process the pain, hurts, and wounds of your life with God and another person.

Blessed are the meek for they shall inherit the earth
- Pray for the ability to have meekness: great strength and direction under the total control of God the Holy Spirit.
- Pray that you remain calm, flexible, and adaptable no matter what.
- Pray that you will make thoughtful requests and wise expressions rather than anger and frustration.

Blessed are those who hunger and thirst after righteousness for they shall be satisfied
- Pray for a new hunger and thirst for righteousness.
- Pray that God would strengthen your desire for good works and the right.
- Pray that God would show you new areas for righteous action.
- Pray that you would lose interest in the wrong, the silly, and the coarse.

Blessed are the merciful for they shall receive mercy
- Pray that God develops in you a new level of mercy and love.
- Pray that you would be sensitive to the perspectives, feelings, and position of others.
- Pray that God would develop a new love for those who deeply hurt and offend you.
- Pray that God gives you eyes to see the second-mile opportunities.

Blessed are the pure in heart for they shall see God
- Pray that God would develop a pure heart within you.
- Pray that God would give you a new ability to evaluate the influences in your life -- good and bad.
- Pray that God gives you the ability to eliminate negative influences.
- Pray that God gives you new desire and ability to turn away from lust.

Blessed are the peacemakers for they shall be called the sons of God
- Pray that God would make you a peacemaker to those around you.

- Pray that God would give you insights into building a common perspective between people at odds.
- Pray that you would choose relationships over things.

Blessed are those who have been persecuted for the sake of righteousness for theirs is the kingdom of heaven

- Pray that you would take a stand for moral righteousness.
- Pray that your faith grows enough that others see it.
- Pray that your faith takes enough action that wicked people will be uncomfortable.
- Pray that many people would want to hear the gospel because of the way you live your life.
- Pray that you would be willing to suffer for the name of Christ.

Day 29: Doctrine

One of the key things that Christian's must learn is to grow in the grace and knowledge of our Lord Jesus Christ. This means that Christians must learn the fundamental truths that undergird reality. Pray that God gives you insight into the ten foundational truths of Christianity so you can build your life upon them.

God; Jesus; Holy Spirit; Mankind; Sin; Salvation; Church; Angels; After Life: Heaven, Hell, and Judgment day; The Return of Christ

God
- Pray that you begin to understand more of the truth of who God is from the Scriptures. How transcendent and awesome is the Almighty God you worship.

Jesus
- Pray that you will come to love the Lord Jesus Christ, the second member of the Trinity who left His place in heaven, who was born as a helpless human baby, lived a perfect life, and voluntarily gave up His life for the sins of the whole world that we might have a relationship with God.

Holy Spirit
- Ask God to give you greater sensitivity to the guidance and wisdom of the Holy Spirit.

Mankind
- Ask God to give you greater insight into the wonder and ugliness of mankind. We are the image bearers of God, and we are carriers of sin and rebellion.

Sin
- Ask God to help you see the depths of selfishness, rebellion, and disobedience in your own heart and in everyone else's heart

Salvation
- Thank God and ask Him for deeper understanding of the process of your salvation and salvation in general.

Church
- Ask God to bless the assembly of Christians to which you belong.
- Ask God to bless the advance of the Church into every place.

Angels
- Ask God to protect you and assist you with His Holy Angels.
- Ask God to help you realize that there is a spiritual war going on between mankind and angels.

After Life: Heaven, Hell, and Judgment day
- Ask God to make heaven, hell, and judgment day real to you.
- Ask God for deeper insights into heaven.
- Ask God for greater understanding of hell.
- Ask God for a constant realization of how everything you think, do, or say will be known on judgment day.

Return of Christ
- Ask God to help you understand more about the return of Christ and those days that are coming in the future.
- Ask God to remind you to live with the reality that He could come at any moment.

Day 30: God

The Ten Major Relationship of Life

There are ten major relationships in life: God, self, marriage, family, work, church, money, society, friends, and enemies. Each of these relationships is crucial to our functioning as Christians. God has directed us in each of these areas and wants us to seek His face about our decisions, actions, thoughts, and plans in each of these relationships.

God

- Ask God to show you at least fifteen ways you need Him today.
- Ask God to show you the spiritual disciplines you need to practice to reignite your love for Him. Circle the ones you want to start:
  - Confession
  - Guidance and wisdom from the Holy Spirit
  - Bible study
  - Prayer
  - Worship – church and personal
  - Fellowship with mentors
  - Fellowship with believers at the same stage of spiritual development
  - Fellowship with new Christians
  - Biblical meditation and memorization
  - Baptism
  - Communion
  - Witnessing
  - Fasting
  - Solitude
  - Service: daily, church, community
  - Love

- o Tithing: Giving a tenth of your income to support the Lord's work
- o Offering: Giving above the tithe for charitable purposes

- Ask God to show you which spiritual disciplines you need to do daily and
  - Which ones weekly
  - Which ones monthly
  - Which ones quarterly
  - Which ones yearly

- Ask God to show you what He knows and you do not know that you need to know today.
- Ask God to show you the problems you have that you will never solve without His wisdom.
- Ask God to show you the areas that you need His strength to do what you know you need to.
- Ask God to show you how you need your spouse, family, work, church, society, and friends.
- Tell God five ways that you need Him spiritually.
- Tell God five ways that you need Him mentally.
- Tell God five ways that you need Him emotionally.
- Tell God five ways that you need Him physically.
- Tell God five ways that you need Him relationally.
- Tell God five ways that you need Him financially.
- Ask God to point out the impossible thing that He wants you to do for Him that you have been avoiding because without God it is impossible.

Day 31: Personal Goals

Relational Goals

Which relationships need to begin, improve, change, or end in order to maximize these major righteous relationships? Ask God for those insights, energy, and mercy.

Ask God about all of the major relationships of your life:
* God
* Self
* Romance
* Family
* Work
* Church
* Finances
* Friends
* Society
* Enemies

What do you need to do to strengthen each of these relationships in a righteous direction?

Spiritual Goals
* Ask God to deepen your perception of Him and your relationship with Him.
* Pray about the development of a consistent spiritual life that gets closer and closer to God as the years go by.

Mental Goals
* Ask God to help you accomplish the full development of your mind in whatever ways are appropriate.
* Pray about all the education you need, both formal schooling and practical training.

Emotional Goals
- Ask God to show you how to fully express your emotions and receive the positive emotions of others.
- Ask God to show you the how, what, who, when, why, and where of this crucial area.

Physical Goals
- Ask God to show you or give you the way to be maximally healthy.
- Pray about everything connected to what God shows you and directs you toward. Write it down.

Financial Goals
- Ask God to help you determine and achieve your financial goals.

Vocational Goals
- Ask God to help you understand and achieve your maximal potential vocationally.

Day 32: Romance/Marriage

Marriage

If you are a husband...

- Pray that you would be a godly husband to your wife.
- Pray that you would meet your wife's top needs.
- Honor: Ask God to show you new ways to add value to your wife.
- Understanding: Ask God to show you new aspects of your wife that you need to understand.
- Security: Ask God to give you practical ways to increase her security.
- Building unity: Ask God to give you the energy and insight to build a new level of unity into your marriage.
- Agreement: Ask God to show you how to discuss the issues of your marriage so that you would come to agreement.
- Nurture: Ask God to give you new insights on how to minister to your spouse's deepest needs.
- Defender: Ask God to help you protect your spouse from destructive forces around her.

If you are a wife...

- Pray that you would be a godly wife to your husband.
- Respect: Ask God to give you a new level of respect for your husband.
- Sexual fulfillment: Ask God to give you a physical desire for your husband.

- Recreational companionship: Ask God to show you how you can meet your husband's need for companionship.
- Non-reactive listening: Ask God to give you a new ability to control your emotions when your husband shares his dreams.
- Adaptation: Ask God to give you a new energy and insight into how to adapt to your husband in the areas of his strengths and weakness so that your marriage would be whole.
- Domestic support: Ask God to show you how to be a more complete answer for your husband's need for domestic support.
- Pray that both you and your spouse would move to the deepest levels of intimacy.
- Pray that both of you would have the energy to really listen – understand -- validate -- what the other person said.
- Pray that you would understand and support each other as you are not seeking to change the unalterable temperament of the other person.
- Pray that your finances would be a powerful testimony to the Christian life.
- Pray that your kids would be an honor in how they act, speak, and conduct themselves.
- Pray that God would highlight areas of personal development that need to be worked on: anger, addictions, relationships, relatives.
- Pray that your marriage would be a testimony of the intimacy between Christ and God.

If you are single…

If you believe that you will be married someday then pray for yourself that you would become the kind of person who would be a good mate. The following qualities are key to becoming a person who could marry well and being a partner who gives and receives love in a healthy way.

Self-Acceptance
- Pray that you would accept and embrace who God has made you and who He has not made you to be.

Humility
- Pray that you would not need to be the center of attention and would be teachable.

Responsibility
- Pray that you would learn to take responsibility for your actions and would become a person others can count on.

Authority-Submission
- Pray that you would learn to adapt to others and be appropriately submissive to others' needs.

Righteousness
- Pray that you would develop a deep desire for what is right instead of what you want with a willingness to sacrifice to accomplish it.

Forgiveness
- Pray that you would develop the ability to forgive people who wrong you, not seeking vengeance against them and learning to love them.

Purity
- Pray that you would develop a pure mind and heart, filling your thoughts with positive and pure images instead of perversions of God's designs.

Peacemaker
- Pray that you learn how to create a peaceful environment and how to live in harmony with other people's lives.

Mature Christian
- Pray that you develop a willingness to suffer for what is right and for Christ.

Day 33: Family

Family

- Ask God for a righteous family: great kids and lots of love- producing righteous acts.

Respect

- Ask God that you and your children would respect: authority, age, nature, and people.
- Ask God to show you something positive you can praise and respect your kids for every day.

Responsibility

- Ask God that you and your children would take full responsibility for their words, actions, attitudes, thoughts, and motives.

Rules

- Ask God to reinforce the boundaries that protect you and your children from violating the laws of God.
- Ask God to help you set up reasonable rules that will help your family have an identity but not be so rigid as to drive your children away.

Relationship

- Ask God to develop a deep emotional bond between you and your children.
- Ask God to show you new ways to make a deeper and lasting emotional bond within your family.

Day 34: Work

- Pray that God would cause you to see your work as employment from God.
- Pray that God would strengthen you to work with a whole heart the whole day.
- Pray that your work would stand out as a testament to a great God to the non Christians around you.
- Pray that you would recognize obedience and submission as a key factor of any great work.
- Pray that you would realize that you present your work every day to the Ancient of Days.
- Present your work to God in a short formal way at the end of each completed section or project.
- Pray that God would strengthen your ability to love people at your work.

Day 35: Friends

- Pray blessings into the lives of your friends. Ask for specific righteous things to take place. Pray for what your friends really need – not just what they may want.
- Ask God to give you more acquaintances.
- Pray that you would find the places where people you would like to become friends with would hang out.
- Pray that you would be more outgoing and talk to potential acquaintances.
- Ask God to give you more causal friends.
- Pray that God would direct you to interests and activities where you could connect with potential casual friends.
- Ask God to give you deeper close friends.
- Pray that God gives you the courage to reveal some of your concerns, problems, and needs to your friends to see if they would be willing to be close friends.
- Pray that the right friend is receptive and willing to listen.
- Ask God to give you deeper intimate friends.
- Pray that God would create just the right time and place where you could share your inner concerns, worries, thoughts, and feelings with someone you already trust.
- Pray that God would allow you to share your true feelings with a friend who would not think less of you after you have shared your inner self.
- Ask God to make you a better friend.
- Ask God to show you who you need to be an acquaintance, casual, close, and intimate friend with who are not at present in those places.

Day 36: Church

It is crucial to pray for your church, your community of faith. There are five main elements that make a dynamic and life-giving church: evangelism, fellowship, discipleship, worship, and compassion.

- Pray for these five things to happen in your church to an ever great degree.
- Ask God to increase the number of non-Christian seekers who attend your church.
- Ask God to increase the number of people who make professions of faith this month.
- Ask God to show the church how to increase the transformation of the people who attend the church.
- Ask God to show the leaders how to increase the number of people who are worshipping the Lord each week at the church.
- Ask God for a great sincerity and depth of worship each week.
- Ask God to give the leaders insight in how to increase the depth of fellowship at the church.
- Ask God to increase the number of people who serve the Lord outside the church as a witness to His love for the world.
- Ask God to increase the number of people who serve the Lord at the church each week.

Day 37: Enemies

Pray for those who persecute you. Ask God to do specific positive things in their life. If you don't know what to pray, ask them the next time you are with them. "What can I pray about for you?"

- Pray that you will be able to love (meet needs, pursue their soul, please) them in specific ways the next time you are with them.
- Pray that you will be able to speak about their strengths and positive actions. Bless those who curse you.
- Pray that you might be able to do a specific good to them that would make them repent. Love your enemies and do good to those who hate you.
- Ask God whether you should educate them about what they did to offend or oppose you. Luke 17:3 - If you brother sins against you rebuke him and if he repents forgive him.
- Ask God to give you forgiveness for this person so you can move on and not let bitterness invade your heart. Luke 17:3
- Ask God how He wants to bring good out of their opposition or wounds. Romans 8:28

Day 38: Money/Finances

Since money cuts across all the relationships of life, it is itself a relationship. It is the only "thing" that Jesus said rises to the level of a relationship. Therefore we need to operate in a godly fashion in this critical relationship. Any godly money plan requires that all three aspects -- income, management, giving -- of a financial plan be directed in a Godly way. It is important that we realize that God wants us to make our money in a righteous way, to manage it in a righteous way, and to be generous with it in a righteous way.

Income
- Pray that you would see the opportunities to make and receive all the income God wants to give.
- Pray that you would not make so much that you would forget God and that you would not make so little to be tempted to steal and profane His name. Proverbs 30
- Pray that you would be diligent at the work that God gives you to do, so you can provide for yourself, your family, the church, and the needy.
- Pray that God gives you new righteous sources of income.
- Ask God to overcome your natural laziness and also to stop working when you have enough for yourself and your family.
- Pray that God would give you all the finances that you need to meet the needs of yourself, your family, your church, and the needy you are supposed to help.

Management
- Pray that God shows you how to manage your money better.
- Pray that God would strengthen you to say no to impulsive spending.

- Pray that you would stay on top of where your money is going.
- Ask God to develop and/or correct your budget or money spending plan.
- Ask God to show you how to get out of debt.
- Pray that you will not let the love of money cloud your life -- a lot or a little. 1 Timothy 6

Giving

- Pray that you would be generous with money.
- Pray that you would remain tender to groups, individuals, and organizations that need funds.
- Pray that your tithe might be given out of real worship.
- Ask God to point out people you need to help financially.
- Pray that Christians would understand that all of their lives are really to be offerings to the Lord.

Day 39: Community, Region, and Country

- Pray that our country would make laws based upon the Ten Commandments that would protect people and release them to glorify God in their uniqueness.
- Pray that your community would do what needs to be done to create an environment of peace and safety.
- Pray that your region would elect and appoint people who are righteous.
- Pray that those who are corrupt and oppressive would be discovered and removed.
- Pray that a righteous economy can be built that allows everyone to express their creativity and uniqueness.
- Pray that you will be able to participate in civic involvements that will push back the injustice and disorder which is always waiting to rush in.
- Pray that your crimes are solved and victims are restored and comforted.
- Pray that the seeds of corruption, exploitation, and greed will be found and rooted out of the community.
- Pray about your involvement in prevention, compassion, justice, and recovery, etc.
- Pray that God shows you how to make a difference in your neighborhood, community, region, and country.
- Pray these things from Psalms 72 for the President, Governor, Representatives, Mayor, Council Members, and other local elected officials. The word king here could be understood as leader not just the supreme leader. Every society has leaders at various levels. The more those leaders are free of corruption and acting righteously with the best interests of the people in mind, the better the society does.

Psalms 72

GIVE the king Thy judgments, O God,
and Thy righteousness to the king's son.
May he judge Thy people with righteousness,
and Thine afflicted with justice.
Let the mountains bring peace to the people,
and the hills in righteousness.
May he vindicate the afflicted of the people,
save the children of the needy,
and crush the oppressor. Let them fear Thee
while the sun endures, and as long as the
moon, throughout all generations. May he
come down like rain upon the mown grass,
like showers that water the earth. In his days
may the righteous flourish, and abundance of
peace till the moon is no more. May he also
rule from sea to sea, and from the River to the
ends of the earth. Let the nomads of the desert
bow before him; and his enemies lick the dust.
Let the kings of Tarshish and of the islands
bring presents; the kings of Sheba and Seba
offer gifts. And let all kings bow down before
him, all nations serve him. For he will deliver
the needy when he cries for help, the afflicted
also, and him who has no helper. He will have
compassion on the poor and needy, and the
lives of the needy he will save. He will rescue
their life from oppression and violence; and
their blood will be precious in his sight; So
may he live; and may the gold of Sheba be
given to him; and let them pray for him
continually; let them bless him all day long.

*May there be abundance of grain in the earth
on top of the mountains; its fruit will wave like
the cedars of Lebanon; and may those from
the city flourish like vegetation of the earth.
May his name endure forever;
may his name increase as long as the sun
shines; and let men bless themselves by him;
let all nations call him blessed. Blessed be the
LORD God, the God of Israel, Who alone
works wonders. And blessed be His glorious
name forever; and may the whole earth be
filled with His glory. Amen, and Amen.*

Day 40: You have not because you ask not

The apostle James states very clearly that, "You do not have because you do not ask." This day is a chance to tell God all about your life and ask Him for what you think you need.

- What would you like to ask God?

Answers:

Blessings:

Comfort:

Growth:

Relationships:

Insights:

Direction:

Prayers: _____

Answers: _____

Conclusion

Congratulations, you have completed a long period of prayer and are richer and wiser for the experience. What was it like to be able to pray for forty straight days with something new to pray every day? Most likely you found a whole new world of communication with God opened up. Our relationship with God can be improved with increased communication. He has already done all that was needed for a relationship to be possible.

Prayer is a wonderful journey into relationship with God. I find most Christians would love to go deep with God; they just don't know how to do it. Now you have in your hand a tool for going deep with God: forty days of in-depth prayer prompts. Keep going and repeat the prayers that were helpful the last time. Embrace the wonder of talking with God about everything. Get His insights, ask for His help, and let Him fill you with energy and grace.

The Christian life is a life lived with God at His direction. Do not settle for a half-Christian life which only involves doing your best to follow God's instructions. Take the journey of life with God, constantly interacting and learning from Him. Prayer is crucial part of this process.

Please use this prayer guide over and over again. Share it with your friends and take them through this initial process of deep prayer. Ask your small group at church to go through this prayer journey together and see all the discussion and depth it fosters.

Going Deep in Prayer - Part II

This is a second forty-day adventure in prayer as an option and to allow you to continue praying. The classic prayer guides were explored in the previous forty days: The Lord's Prayer, The Ten Commandments, The Fruit of the Spirit, Types of Prayer, and The Beatitudes. This next prayer guide follows the alphabet to move you to pray in directions that you might not normally pray. This way of praying for various topics can take you in unique and powerful directions. It starts with the letter A and gives you two days worth of prayer prompts that begin with the letter A. Then it moves on to two days worth of prayer prompts that start with the letter B. It goes through every letter of the alphabet and gives at least one day, and in most cases, two days worth of prayer prompts.

Obviously you could also create your own alphabetic prayer guide by thinking of topics under each letter of the alphabet that have not been included here.

Day 1: Abundance, Abide, Ability

Prayer guides prompt us to pray about things that we would not normally think to pray about. One of the ways to do this is to take the alphabet and pray one or two things from each of the letters of the alphabet.

Abundance

In John 10:10, Jesus says that He came that we might have an abundant life: Are you praying for it and taking advantage of every opportunity God sends your way? This does not necessarily mean financial abundance although that is not ruled out. We must be alert to the places where God is giving us an opportunity to have more than we need so that we can share with someone else.

Are you alert to what He may be doing to produce it?
- Ask God to give you abundance in every area of life so that you can share with others outside of that relationship.
- Look at the ten relationships where is God giving you an opportunity to produce abundance: God, Self, Marriage, Family, Work, Church, Money, Society, Friends, Enemies.

Abide

In John 15, Jesus tells us that true believers abide in Him.
- Pray that you would abide in Christ; that you would love and relate to Christ staying connected to Him and doing nothing to shame Him.

Ability

In Ephesians 2:10, God tells us that we are His workmanship created for good works that God planned before the world began.
- Pray that you would be alert to any abilities that God has put within you that He wants you to use for His glory. Pray that you develop your abilities.

Day 2: Abuse, Academic, Accident

Abuse
- Pray for those who are being spiritual, mentally, emotionally, physically, relationally, and vocationally abused.
- Pray that God would show them the way of escape and that they might take it.

Academic
- Pray for those who are in school.
- Pray that they might expand their mind to glorify God.
- Pray that they will not fall victim to the false ideas and philosophies.
- Pray that they will work hard.
- Pray that they will see the glory of God in the designs they see and knowledge they obtain.

Accident
- Pray for protection against the accidents that are coming. Matthew 19.
- Pray for insight into why certain accidents happened to you.
- Pray for grace and action to turn accidents into blessings – cooperating with God.

Day 3: Backbiting, Backslide, Bait, Bear

Backbiting

Everyone agrees that backbiting is damaging. It is damaging in families. It is damaging at work. It is damaging at church.

- Pray that you would not participate in backbiting.
- Pray that an effective means of limiting and/or eliminating backbiting would be found for your family, work, and church.

Backslide

In 1 John 5:16, we are told to pray for those who have sinned.

- Pray for those who have wandered back into lifestyles of sin, wickedness, and evil. Pray that they will seek the Lord and ask for His forgiveness, wisdom, and help.
- Think of five people you know who have wandered away from God and back into sin. Ask God to draw them back.

1.
2.
3.
4.
5.

Bait

James 1 tells us that sin is like bait to tempt us to move in the wrong direction. Pray that you recognize the worm covered hook. Pray that you resist the bait and turn away from it when it is offered to you.

Bear

In Galatians 6, we are told to bear one another's burden and thus fulfill the law of Christ.

- Pray that God gives you grace, power, and mercy to bear the burdens of those you love.

- Pray that you have the courage not to bear but to expose the immoral burdens of others.

Day 4: Barrier, Battle, Beauty

Barrier

- Ask God for wisdom that you may erect barriers between yourself and the sins that you are most likely to commit. This is so that when you are at a weak moment and want to sin, you still will have to climb over a barrier and this will deter you from sin in your moment of weakness.

- Look at the seven deadly sins and acknowledge the three to four sins that you are most inclined to do. Then write down barriers that would keep you from doing them in a weak moment.
    Pride
    Envy
    Anger
    Lust
    Sloth
    Gluttony
    Greed

Battle

In 1 Peter 5:8, we are told that Satan prowls about like a roaring lion seeking whom he may devour. In Ephesians 6:18-31, we are told that we have a spiritual struggle against the spiritual forces of wickedness that rebelled from God. Therefore we should pray that we are alert as to the battle raging around us.

- Pray that God would open your eyes to see the battle and to be kept from being captured and held in an enemy prisoner of war camp.
- Pray that you see the righteous actions that you can take to bring victory to Christ's camp.

Beauty

- Praise God for the beauty that you see around you.
- Realize that the Devil likes to hijack beauty to lure people into sin and destruction, so pray for discernment regarding the beauty around you.

Day 5: Call, Callous, Calm

Call

God is calling believers to serve Him. He is asking them to use their gifts, talents, abilities, and skills for the kingdom of God. Some people do that full time in a vocational way and most people do that as a part-time volunteer at churches, charities, and righteous organizations.

- Pray that you would hear God's call to serve Him in various ways.

I think that God may be calling me to serve Him in these ways:
1.
2.
3.
4.
5.

Callous

In Ephesians 4:19, God says that it is possible for a person to repeatedly sin and make their conscience callous and unresponsive to the promptings of God.

- Pray that any callousness in your conscience would be removed and you would be able to sense the conviction and guidance of the Holy Spirit.

Calm

One of the key ingredients in meekness is the ability to remain calm when things are not going as you have planned or expected.

- Pray for a godly calmness that realizes that God is sovereign and still in control. Even when things are not going the way you want, God has not lost control of the world.

Day 6: Calvary, Carnal, Camaraderie, Careful

Calvary

- Praise God for the work that Christ did at Calvary through the death of His only begotten Son, Jesus Christ.

Carnal

In Galatians 5:19-21, we are told about the deeds of the flesh. These actions which arise from our sinful nature want us to pay attention to selfish desires.

- Pray that you will not do what your flesh wants but will instead be instantly obedient to the promptings of the Holy Spirit.

Camaraderie

The Psalms state that it is good when brothers dwell together in unity.

- Pray that your family, your work, and your church will develop a new encouraging camaraderie. Ask God for insights as to how you can move that along.

Careful

In Philippians 4:6,7, we are told to be anxious or full of care over nothing.

- So give all your concerns to God and tell Him how you would like things to work out. Do not be full of care, anxiety, and worry.

Day 7: Dad

Jesus makes a repeated point of presenting God as our heavenly Father, as our Dad. There are probably many things that you would like to say to your Dad, so go ahead and say them. This is called praying. The speaking of the questions is very helpful and can begin a dialogue between you and your heavenly Father. Let me assure you that God is not afraid of your questions. Jeremiah the prophet asked very tough and emotionally laden questions. Job asked tough questions.

Why did You…?

Why didn't You…?

Where were You when…?

How did You…?

What were You thinking when…?

How come…?

Who sinned to cause…?

Why would You allow…?

When am I going to…?

When are You going to…?

Day 8: Damage

In Genesis 3, sin entered the world and therefore we live in a sinful broken world where damage is a part of how and where we live. We can pray for healing. We can also be a part of the healing and repair of damage.

- Pray for five damaged areas in your life that you would be healed. Pray for sensitivity to what part you need to play in healing and repairing your damage.

1.

2.

3.

4.

5.

- Pray for five people you know whose damaged areas would be healed. Pray for the five people that they will be alert to their part in the healing and repair of their damage.

1.

2.

3.

4.

5.

Day 9: Ecclesiastes, Economy, Educate

Ecclesiastes

The book of Ecclesiastes was written to keep people from spending their life on vain pursuits. Don't waste your life on becoming an expert at things that don't really matter.

- Pray that God will help you see through the vanity of what the world has to offer.
- Pray that you would make the difference that God wants you to make in people's lives.

Economy

The Bible tells us to work hard that we will have enough to share with those in need. Believers must contribute to the larger economy in a different way than most people in the world. We are working not just for ourselves and our families but for the opportunity to be an instrument of love in the Lord's hand.

- Pray that you will find areas where you can produce a surplus.
- Pray that you will recognize your opportunities to share when they come.

Educate

We are all to teach others how to live the life of a Christian. Our lives educate as much, if not more than, our words.

- Pray that you are accurately teaching the Christian way.
- Pray that when you do teach, you will be glorifying to God.

We also must continue to be educated in the way of Christ. How do we love to abundance in every area of life? Mark 12:30,31

- Ask God for wisdom and do what He tells you.

Day 10: Effectual, Ego-Centric, Elect

Effectual

James 5 tells us the effectual fervent prayer of a righteous man accomplishes much. Are your prayers accomplishing lots of things in other people's lives and in your own? If not, how can you be more effectual in your prayers?

- Pray that you will know how to pray more accurately for the will of God.
- Pray that you will eliminate anything from your life that reduces your ability to be effectual in prayer.
- Ask God to use you to accomplish things so that people will acknowledge God and glorify Him.

Ego-centric

- Pray that your ego does not get in the way of what God wants to do through you.
- Pray that you care about others more than you care about yourself.
- Ask God what you need to do to help others succeed.

Elect

Before the world ever began the Scriptures tell us that God chose those who would be in His family. He could have chosen any criteria as the basis for His Sovereign choice of who will enjoy heaven and intimate relationship with Him. Scripture tells us that His choice of us involves our belief and trust in Him. John 3:16. Most people believe that He chose those who would respond back to His offer of love and forgiveness. Celebrate the wonder of God's choice of you. Remember, He did not have to choose anyone on this rebellious planet, and yet He chose to redeem a people for Himself.

Day 11: Evangelism

- Tell God in prayer that you are willing to share your faith in this next week if He brings someone up to you and asks you. If He does not have someone ask you then you don't have to share.

- List ten people who you would like to see become Christian. Then pray for them that God would draw them to Himself and they would respond to the gospel.

1.

2.

3.

4.

5.

6.

7.

8.

9.

10.

Day 12: Fail, Faith, Fallacy

Fail

Every spiritual person that God uses in the Scriptures goes through periods of failure and incompetence. It is not whether you fail, it is whether you continue to have faith in God, continue to push towards a righteous goal, and are willing to learn from your failures.

- Pray that God will encourage you and teach you through each of your failures.

Faith

The Scriptures state that it is faith that grasps the promises and righteousness of God, not our works. It is the person who trusts God for salvation and trusts God as He directs during our lives that is approved by Him.

- Tell God that you trust Him to supply forgiveness and salvation through the death of Jesus Christ for you. You are trusting Jesus Christ alone for salvation and not leaning on your own works.
- Pray that you would clearly understand what God is asking you to trust Him to do.

Fallacy

The Scriptures state that there are many people in the world who are trying to take people's minds captive through false reasoning and fallacy.

- Ask God that you would see fallacious arguments when they are offered.
- Pray that you would help others see the fallacy of trusting in anything other than Christ.

Day 13: Fame, Family, Fast

Fame

In 1 John 2:15-18, the Scriptures tell us to not fall for the promises of fame. It is a trick and will not really satisfy.

- Pray that you would not give in to the temptations of the flesh, the temptations of the eyes, or the boastful pride of life.

The Scriptures also tell us that we can desire the fame of knowing God deeply.

- Therefore pray that God will teach you His ways and His truth so that you can boast of your knowledge of Him.

Family

- Pray for your family that has not become Christian.
- Pray for your family that once knew Christ but is wandering from Him.
- Pray for your family that they will be strong Christians and productive members of society.
- Pray that you will be able to lovingly inject righteousness into your family.
- Pray that you will retain the righteous patterns your family taught you.
- Pray that you will understand and change the unhealthy patterns your family taught you.

Fast

The Scriptures repeatedly talk about fasting as a way to increase the power of prayer.

- Today: skip a meal and pray instead of eat. Pour out your heart to the Lord.

Day 14: Gain, Gather, Generous

Gain

In Philippians 3:14, God tells us that we are to press on to the goal of the prize of the upward call of God in Christ Jesus. The goal for the Christian is to glorify God maximally, using all that He made you to be.

- Ask God how you can achieve that goal during this year.
- Ask God how to get started glorifying Him more during this week.

Gather

The Scriptures consistently encourage Christians to gather together to share burdens, to encourage one another, and to build up one another. Hebrews 10:25

- Ask God to gather new people around you that will encourage you and you can encourage.
- Ask God to draw people to your church that they might find Christ and be built up in Him.

Generous

God is trying to build a person who is generous in spirit, faith, friendship, and treasure.

- Ask God to root out your needless selfishness and show you how to become a person with a generous spirit.
- Ask God for discernment as to where to be generous with your finances.
- Ask God to direct you where to be generous with your time and talents.

Day 15: Gentle, Genuine, Gird

Gentle
In most of the lists of qualities that God is trying to produce in the Christian, the word gentleness or meekness appears. Gentleness is an absence of harshness and rudeness; a person who is easy to be around.
- Pray that God would give you an abundance of gentleness.
- Ask God to show you the ways that you come across harsh or rude.

Genuine
An authentic person is the same person in private that they are in public.
- Ask God to make the hidden person the same as the public person – full of grace, truth, and righteousness.
- Ask God to show you how you are pretending to be something you shouldn't and/or that you aren't.
- Ask God to let you remove the mask, letting the right people in at the right time so they can encourage, love, and comfort you.

Gird
In Ephesians 6:18-31, God tells us to gird up our loins with truth.
- Ask God to show you the truths that you need in order to resist the attacks of the Devil.
- Ask God to give you a way of embracing and retaining the key truths you need.
- Take up in prayer the truths of the Scriptures so that in spite of what you feel or hear, you can resist the impulses of the Devil.

Day 16: Habitual, Hades, Hand

Habitual

Godliness is defined in the ancient world as a group of spiritual practices that one consistently or habitually performs to bring one close to God. In Christianity one does not earn God's favor by habitual practices, but we do draw near to Him through the habitual practice of righteous spiritual disciplines.

* Pray that you will add the right habitual practices to your daily routine so that you will be constantly conversing and interacting with the Spirit of the Living God.

Hades

The Scripture states that hell or Hades is a real spiritual place where people who are unwilling to let God forgive their sins end up. There truly is a heaven to gain and a hell to lose. Spend some time thinking about those who are right now rejecting Christ and choosing to go their own independent way.

* Ask God for the opportunity to tell them about the wonder of forgiveness and acceptance in God's family through faith.

Hand

In 1 Corinthians 12-14, the Scriptures remind us that we are now the hands and feet of Jesus Christ in the world. The only Jesus that the world sees is what we do.

* Ask God what He wants you to do to show love to your neighbors.
* Ask God what He wants you to do to show love to your region.
* Ask God what He wants you to do to show love to your world.

Day 17: Holy, Hazard, Harass

Holy

In 1 Peter 1, the apostle calls upon Christians to be holy as God is holy. We are to be pure and separated from sin.

- Ask God to show you any areas where you are clinging to sin and it is affecting your ability to live for Him.
- Ask God to show you the way to move away from any sins that still cling to you.

Hazard

It is clear from the Lord's Prayer and other places in Scripture that the world is not a safe place. There are hazards that will damage and even destroy us. We need to know where they are and how to avoid them.

- Pray that God will show you where the hazards are in your life so you can mark them
- Ask God to show you how to avoid falling into them. Do what He tells you.

Harass

The name of the being we call Devil means accuser, slanderer, harasser. He has assigned wicked spirits to harass you. Their job is to accuse you to God, to others, and to yourself. You must stay vigilant so as not to believe the endless stream of accusations that come in your direction. If you are doing anything good or will do something good, you will be harassed.

- Ask God to remind you that righteous actions will always get harassed.
- Ask God to give you the strength to focus on the Lord Jesus and not the harasser and slanderer.
- Ask God to cover you with a force field of His love so that their comments have no impact.

Day 18: Ideal: Beatitudes

Ideal

Beatitudes: Lord, I agree with you that the Beatitudes are the ideal and how I want to express myself to others.

Recite these as prayers that you want the Lord to make true in your life. When you recite these truths as though they were already a part of your life, you may notice that it sets up a difference between what you are presently and what you want to be. This is good. If you pray this prayer over and over again, you will find God moving you more in the direction of the truths of this prayer.

- **Blessed are the poor in Spirit for theirs is the kingdom of heaven:** I am aware of how I need God and the others. I am teachable and I do not need to be the center of attention.

- **Blessed are those who mourn for they shall be comforted:** I take the time to grieve the losses and pain in my life, and I do not make excuses or cover up my failures and shortcomings.

- **Blessed are the meek for they shall inherit the earth:** I am flexible and calm when my expectations are not met, and I make thoughtful requests and wise adaptations.

- **Blessed are those who hunger and thirst after righteousness for they shall be satisfied:** I have a burning desire to see the right things done, and I know the righteous cause(s) God wants me to promote.

- **Blessed are the merciful for they shall receive mercy:** I forgive and look for second-mile opportunities to overcome feelings of vengeance.

- **Blessed are the pure in heart for they shall see God:** I make sure that my core thoughts and images are pure and positive.

- **Blessed are the peacemakers for they shall be called the sons of God:** I help others stop making war with each other and help them live in harmony with each other and God.

- **Blessed are those who have been persecuted for righteousness for theirs is the kingdom of heaven:** I stand up for what is right even if it is inconvenient and costly.

- **Blessed are you when men revile you and persecute you and say all manner of evil against you falsely on account of Me. Rejoice and be exceedingly glad, for so they persecuted the prophets who were before you:** I openly identify with Jesus and some people are offended by that.

Day 19: Ideal: Fruit of the Spirit

Fruit of the Spirit

Lord, I agree with you that the fruit of the spirit are how I want to live. Recite these as prayers that you want the Lord to make true in your life. When you recite these truths as though they were already a part of your life, you may notice that it sets up a difference between what you are presently and what you want to be. This is good. If you pray this prayer over and over again, you will find God moving you more in the direction of the truths of this prayer.

Every day I am alert to God's impulses

- **Love:** I meet needs, pursue other's soul, and please people.

- **Joy:** I deepen my relationships and am positive with others.

- **Peace:** I do not fight with people and live in harmony with them.

- **Patience:** I keep persevering toward a righteous goal.

- **Kindness:** I am pleasant, helpful, merciful, and encouraging.

- **Goodness:** I am benefiting others.

- **Meekness:** I am flexible and calm. I make thoughtful requests and wise adaptations.

- **Faithfulness:** I stay the righteous course.

- **Self-Control:** I moderate my desires.

    Against such things there is no law

Day 20: Identify, Ignorance

Identify

The Scriptures make it clear that believers are to identify with Christ more than any other aspect of their lives. Jesus has asked Christians to be baptized, to take Communion, and to witness to others about their faith in Christ.

- Ask God to give you the chance to identify with Christ this week. Let Him know that you are ready to share your faith in Christ.
- Ask Him to bring someone up to you and ask you a question about your faith and you will identify with Christ.

Ignorance

In 2 Peter 3:8, the Scriptures tell us to grow in the grace and knowledge of our Lord and Savior Jesus Christ. Christians understand that basic reality is outlined in the ten basic doctrines of the Christian faith: God, Jesus, Holy Spirit, Man, Sin, Salvation, Church, Angels, Afterlife, The Return of Christ. The average believer today has a very thin knowledge of these things, and it allows them to be driven and tossed by every wind of teaching and rumor.

- Pray that God would direct you to a good Bible Study, book, or teacher who can deepen your understanding of these crucial concepts.
- Ask God to encourage your church to offer more classes in truly understanding the Christian world view.

Day 21: Jealous, Jeremiah, Journal

Jealous

In James 4, the Scriptures tell us that the Lord is jealous for us. He is rightly possessive towards those who have committed themselves to Him.

- Ask God to show you the other things that are becoming His rivals for primary place in your life.
- Pray that you will reprioritize your life before God acts to help you.

Jeremiah

In Jeremiah 15, the prophet of God got real honest about what seemed like a raw deal. He called God an unreliable stream and a being who doesn't keep His promises. There was an authentic openness and unvarnished anger in Jeremiah's accusations. God can handle our emotions when things don't work out the way we have envisioned and we blame Him. We need to get this vile bitterness out of our minds.

- Pray through all the difficult questions that you have for God.
- Ask Him and tell Him all your emotions. He already knows them, but He wants you to get them out into the open so that they do not fester.
- Get real with God and your faith will grow, not shrink.

Journal

One of the consistent ways that people have prayed to God in deep ways over the centuries is to write out their prayers.

- Write out what you would like to say to God.
- Write out what you want to ask God.
- Write out the insights from Scripture that God is giving you.

Day 22: Journey, Joy, Judge

Journey

Life is a journey and it is not so much the destination that you reach by the end of life but how you have treated the other passengers with you on the journey.

- Ask God to strengthen you to love the people who are around in this part of the journey.
- Ask God to show you the reality of this short journey we call life and how it is not about accumulating and posturing.

Joy

Over and over again the Scriptures entreat us to have joy. We must have joy in order to make it in this world. The power of joy is that it means that you have the Lord's positive outlook on every problem. He does have the answer to every problem. Joy also means deepening relationships with others.

- Ask God to show you His perspective on your current situation so you can be as optimistic as He is.
- Ask God to deepen particular relationships that will increase your joy this month.

Judge

The Scriptures tell us two things about judges: One, do not make judgments unless you are in that position. Second, when asked to make judgments, we must make impartial righteous ones that benefit all involved.

- Ask God to stop you from trying to pick the log out of your brother's eye when you still have a log coming out of your own.

Day 23: Kill, Kind, Knock

Kill

The Scriptures state clearly that, "Thou shall not kill." It extends the commandment beyond just physical killing to spiritual killing by outlawing witchcraft and false religions; mental killing by outlawing scheming against a person's goods and planning vengeance; emotional killing by outlawing swearing, cursing, and verbal abuse; and relational killing by outlawing slander and the treating of the alien and stranger differently.

- Pray that you would not be guilty of killing physically by the use or threat of violence to get your way.
- Pray that you would not be guilty of killing spiritually through curses, vengeance, scheming against them.
- Pray that you would not be guilty of killing emotionally through swearing, cursing, and verbal assault.
- Pray that you would not be guilty of killing relationally by stereotyping, slander, prejudice, and discrimination.
- Pray for the people that are being physically, spiritually, emotionally, and relationally killed.
- Ask God what you can do to stop even one of these "killings."

Kind

One of the fruit of the spirit is kindness. Pleasant helpfulness is prompted by God's Spirit in almost every week of your life.
- Listen to the prompting of the Holy Spirit to be pleasantly helpful.
- Ask God for the strength to be pleasantly helpful when you don't feel like it.

Knock

Jesus says that if we knock then the door will be opened to us.

What closed doors exist in your life that really should be open in order for you to pursue your dream and God's goals?
What doors do you need to have opened so that you can pursue your righteous dreams?

- Pray that those doors would open for you. Do not give up on your dream.

Day 24: Kindred, Know, Kudos

Kindred

We all are a part of a family and an extended family structure. We can and should pray that our family would become Christian and that they would grow in the grace and knowledge of the Lord Jesus Christ.

- Pray for those family members who are not Christians that they would become Christian.

1.
2.
3.
4.
5.

- Pray that those who are Christian would begin living out the testimony of Christ.
- Pray for each family member in terms of their living out God's truths in each of their relationships.
- Ask God to point out which of their relationships need the most prayer.

Know

The Scriptures constantly prod us to know more about God and how to live life God's way. What don't you know about how to handle life? What areas of life constantly cause problems for you: Finances, Parenting, Temptation, Romance, Family, Career, Enemies.

- Ask God to begin educating you about these areas.
- You are ready to listen.
- You are ready to begin acting differently than you have in the past.

Kudos

When you see a turtle on a fence post, you know that it didn't get there by itself. So everything that you have accomplished in your life has been the result of a lot of people's help and encouragement. Yes, you made some right choices but there are always people to thank.

- Ask God to bring to your mind who you should honor and thank for the good things in your life.
- Write down the names that God brings to your mind.
- Write them a note.
- Make a phone call.
- Send them a letter.

Day 25: Lack, Lament, Last

Lack

Many people are motivated by a lack of something that they do not know how to completely fulfill.

* Ask God to show you where you lack all that He wants to give you.
* Ask God to show you the misplaced and dysfunctional ways you have tried to make up for that lack.
* Ask God to fill up your lack with His answers, His relationships, and His joy.

Lament

The second beatitude tells us that the person who mourns their pain, wrongs, and wounds is blessed because they will be comforted. Unfortunately our culture tells you to hide, avoid, and deny the pains of your past. But Jesus is always right. We need to grieve, lament, mourn, cry, and process our pain, whether we caused it or someone else did it to us. We live in a sinful, broken world where things are not as they should be.

* Ask God to grieve with you, mourn with you, and process with you as you interact with the difficult things in your life.
* Ask God to send you someone who will listen as you go through this process.

Last

One of the last things that will happen is the Return of Christ. This is called the Blessed Hope of the believer. Jesus and the apostles tell us to keep this wonderful event in our minds as it could happen at any moment. He says that He wants His servants to be found faithful when He returns. What would being found faithful look like for you?

- Ask God what He wants you to be doing when He returns.
- Ask yourself what you need to stop doing so He doesn't find you doing it when He returns.
- Ask God to remind you that He could return today.

Day 26: Lasciviousness, Laugh, Lavish

Lasciviousness

The Scriptures declare that one of the deeds of the flesh is lasciviousness. This is stirring up our sensual appetites so that lust begins to dominate our thoughts. Our world, our flesh, and the Devil are all interested in lascivious activities. We must be equally ready with ways to not go down that road and to get off that road if we ever start down that road.

- Ask God for numerous realistic ideas to keep you from moving towards lascivious thoughts and activities.
- Write these down and begin implementing them.
- Ask God for realistic ways to stop if you do start moving in a lustful, sensual, and lascivious direction.

Laugh

It is clear from the teaching of Jesus that He understood humor. He could tell an exaggerated tale and turn a very funny phrase. We need to have laughter and love in our life.

- Ask God to inject more righteous laughter in your life.
- Ask God to let you be a source of joy and laughter in other people's life.
- Ask God to show you how to add more righteous lightheartedness in your life.

Lavish

The Scriptures tell that God has lavished His grace upon us through His Son. Are you enjoying the full measure of the grace of God and taking full advantage of His lavish grace?

- Ask God to show you more of the power and riches of the grace of God that can be active in your life.
- Ask God to show you how to use the grace of God to bless your life even more.

Day 27: Missionaries, Main-Thing, Marriage, Magnify, Maid

Missionaries

- Pray for missionaries that you know personally
- Pray for the missionaries regarding their families, safety, health, closeness with the Lord, food, finances, and equipment needs.
  - Pray for countries that God puts on your heart.
  - Pray for evangelism in hard to reach areas.
  - Pray for spiritual strength and spiritual discernment.
  - Put on each piece of armor of God for them.

1.
2.
3.
4.
5.
6.
7.
8.
9.
10.

Main-Thing

One of the most difficult things to do in life is to keep the main thing the main thing. In every relationship there is a main thing, and we can get all caught up in doing everything else other than the main thing.

- Ask God to help you see what is the main thing in each area of life and how to keep the proper focus on it.
- Ask God to show you how to make significant progress on the main project in the key relationships of life.

Marriage

In various places in the Scriptures, God tells the husband to minister to the needs of his wife and the wife to minister to the needs of her husband.

- Pray that God would make you sensitive to the needs of your spouse even though they are different than yours.
- Ask God to show you how to meet one need of your spouse today in a new way.
- Ask God to increase the fun and joy in your marriage.

If you are not married but want to be married someday...

- Ask God to increase the qualities in your life which would make you a great mate.
- Ask God to also increase the qualities in your future spouse.

If you are not married and do not see yourself being married...

- Pray for the people around you who are married that their commitment to each other would become stronger and that they would start loving each other at a new level and intensity.

Magnify

List ten ways that you can magnify God in your life this week.

1.   6.

2.   7.

3.   8.

4.   9.

5.   10.

Maid

We all resist being someone's maid, yet the Scriptures call upon Christians to have a servant's heart.

- Ask God who you should serve today to let them know that God loves them

Day 28: Maintenance, Malcontent, Malign, Management, Murder, Mask

Maintenance

All of our lives are full of things and relationships that need to be maintained. Many times we ignore the little maintenance issues that would allow that thing or relationship to work smoothly.

- Ask God to bring to your mind the little things that you should do to make the things and the relationships in your life work well. Write down what comes to mind to let Him know that you are paying attention.

Malcontent

We live in a broken, sinful world where things are not as they should be. Often our lives are so busy just trying to get by that we do not take notice of the broken things that should be fixed. But each of us can make a difference in our sinful world by insisting on righteousness in some area by injecting righteousness into a broken thing and making it right.

- Ask God to show you the broken thing that you should be malcontented about because you can make a difference.
- There is often an organization already going that will help you accomplish a measure of righteousness in a direction.

Malign

Often people will malign you and insult you to just get ahead. The words that they say stick in your mind and heart for a long time.

- Ask God to wash those words out of your mind.
- Ask God to build walls of protection around you so that the slanderous things that others are saying will not hurt you.
- Ask God to let you forgive the people who have wounded you in the past.

Management

- Pray for those who help manage your life.
- Pray for the government agencies and officials that they would pursue righteous goals and not selfish ends.
- Pray for the city officials and the initiatives that they put forth, that they would truly benefit others and not just enrich the few.
- Pray for police officers that they would be protected when they confront evil.
- Pray for bosses at work that they would have the best interest of those they direct in their mind.

Murder

- Pray for those who are right now thinking about committing murder as the way out of a problem.
- Pray that God would stop them and that they would turn away from this possibility.
- Pray that those who are looking at using violence or the threat of violence to get their way would be stopped or stop themselves.
- Pray that those who emotionally murder people through disrespect, prejudice, arrogance, discrimination, etc., would realize what they are doing and be convicted enough to stop.

Mask

- Pray the people in your church will be able to drop their Christian masks with each other and ask for prayer, tell each other when they are hurting, comfort one another, and strengthen one another.
- Pray that there is the liberty in the church to live without masks and enjoy the freedom to be oneself.

Day 29: Name, Nativity, New, Needs, Neighbor

Name

Proverbs says that a person's name is of great importance.

- Pray for your reputation that people will know you as an honest, truthful, and quality person
- Ask God to make you aware of how you can repair your reputation if you have damaged it.

Nativity

- Thank God for sending the Son of God to become a human baby so that He could completely identify with mankind, live a perfect life, and then voluntarily give up that life to pay for our sins and the sins of the whole world.
- Spend some time being amazed that the second person of the Trinity was willing to become a helpless human baby cared for by flawed, sinful human parents in order to have the joy of fellowship with sinful people.

New

- Pray for new things to come into your life.
- Pray for a new view of old things in your life.
- Ask God to show you the steps you need to take to bring a newness and freshness to your life.
- Ask God to supply the new that you need. Get specific as to what it might be. Let Him know that He is more than welcome to substitute something better in the place of what you ask for.

Needs

The Bible says that the Laodicean church in the book of Revelation left their first level of love of Jesus because they did not realize how much they needed Him every day. Take a test of your love of the Savior by thinking, praying, asking, and mediating on the ways that you need the Savior today.

- Write down 15 ways that you need God today.

1.
2.
3.
4.
5.
6.
7.
8.
9.
10.
11.
12
13.
14.
15.

Neighbor

- Pray for your neighbors – take a mental prayer walk and pray for each of the people and families that live around where you live.
- Pray that God would bless them with strong relationships,
- Pray that God would encourage them with work and meaningful activities.
- Pray that God would call them to Himself and that they would have a relationship with Him.

Day 30: Obedient, Obituary, Oblivious, Obstacle, Occasion, Offender, Office, Opportunity, Optimism

Obedient

The Bible says that we should be obedient to the commands and promptings of the Spirit of Christ.

* Ask God to point out where you are not obedient to His commands.
* Ask God to direct you through clear promptings again because you will obey His voice.

Obituary

Because we live in a world where sin has invaded, one day everyone will die unless Jesus returns first. This means that one day you will have an obituary notice in the paper

* Talk with God about what your obituary notice should say about you.
* Talk with God about whether right now it would say positive, significant things about you.
* Ask God what He wants you to do so that your life will count even more.
* Ask God to help you make a difference in other people's lives.

Oblivious

All of us have blind spots in our behavior, manners, and decision making process. These are flaws and dysfunctions in how we operate that keep us from being all we can be for Christ and ourselves.

* Ask God to begin showing you your blind spots so you can take appropriate actions to correct or deal with them.
* Ask God how to begin changing or compensating for the blind spots you uncover.

Obstacle

The being we know as Satan is called that because he places himself in the way as our adversary. He seeks to manipulate people, systems, and things to keep us from accomplishing God's will. There are obstacles in our path to doing God's will.

- Pray about these.
- Ask God to show you the obstacles that are currently in your path that keep you from living the abundant, significant life God has in mind.
- Ask God how to get around, under, over, or through the obstacles in the way of His will.
- Ask God to throw the obstacles out of the way so that you will be able to accomplish His will.
- Ask God to give you the courage to keep going until you are past the obstacle.
- Ask God to keep you from giving up and settling down on this side of the obstacle because it won't move.

Occasion

There is something in our culture that says that an occasion is made by others. But there are all kinds of wonderful moments in our life that really are occasions that need to be celebrated and noted.

- Ask God to point out when something is a significant moment and needs to be turned into an occasion and celebrated.
- Ask God to make you sensitive to the occasions in other people's lives.

Offender

All of us in this sinful, broken world have been or will be hurt, wounded, and victimized. It is a fact of a world gone wrong because of sinful choices.

- Confess to God that offenses and pain will come because of the sinfulness of man.
- Tell God that you want to forgive the people who have wounded you.
- Tell God all about the hurt, pain, and wounds.
- Ask God to flood you with forgiveness and hope so that you can move past the wound.
- Ask God to give you the power to forgive the person so that this person will have no more place in your heart.

Office
- Pray for the people in your office.
- Ask God to bless them; to bless their relationships; to draw them closer to Christ wherever they are now; and to tangibly show His love for them.

Opportunity
- Ask God for eyes to see the opportunities that you should go after:
  - Relationally
  - Financially
  - Spiritually
  - Vocationally
  - Parentally

Optimism
Our God is the God of all hope. No matter how bleak the situation is, there is always hope because of what God can do.
- Ask God to show you the things that you can pin your hope on.
- Ask God to give you an optimistic outlook about what He is doing and will do in the future.
- Ask God to show you clearly how you can participate in building the righteous and hopeful future.

Day 31: Pace, Pain, Papa, Pardon, Parent, Passion, Positive Confession

Pace

- Pray about the pace of your life. Is it sustainable for the long haul?
- Ask God how to build some margins and rest into your life.
- Ask God whether you should speed up or whether you should slow down.

Pain

Jesus says in the second Beatitude that, "Blessed are those who mourn for they shall be comforted." There is a huge need to grieve our losses and wounds, and yet we often hide what happened to us and let our pain fester and grow.

- Tell God of your losses, pains, and wounds. It can be very helpful to do this out loud. Write these feelings and incidents in a journal. Get the issues outside of your head. Sometimes -- if it is safe -- it can be helpful to pray with a friend who can handle all the emotions and issues.

Papa

Talk to God as your heavenly Father

- Tell Him about your relationships: how they're going, what is happening, what is not happening.
- Tell Him about your frustrations.
- Ask Him about the future and the various choices you have.

Pardon

- Thank God for the pardon offered in His Son, Jesus Christ.

- Tell God you are willing to pardon those people who have wronged you because you have been pardoned for so much yourself.

Parent
- Pray for your parents.
- Pray for the parents of little children that you know that they would be wise and loving.
- Pray for the parents of teenagers that they will be able to change their parenting style to match the needs of their teenager.
- Pray for parents of college and work-bound children that they will adjust to the role of counselor and friend.

Passion
- Pray your way through the Stations of the Cross in order to remember the sacrifice that Christ has made on your behalf:

The condemnation of Jesus by Pilate; Jesus' acceptance of the cross; His first fall; The encounter with his mother; *(John 19:25-26)* Simon of Cyrene helping Jesus; *(Matthew 27:32, Mark 15:21, Luke 23:26)* His second fall; The encounter with the women of Jerusalem; *(Luke 23:27-31)* His third fall; Jesus being stripped of his garments; *(Luke 23:34, John 19:23)* The crucifixion; Jesus' death; Jesus' removal from the cross; and The burial of Jesus.

Positive Confession
Confession means to agree with God and His position about something you did, said, or thought about doing. It is often negative, but it can be positive. This time focus on the positive.

Love
- Ask God to remind you of times that you truly loved someone yesterday. Celebrate this and agree with God about it.

Joy
- Ask God to remind you of times that you were truly joyful yesterday. Celebrate this and agree with God about it.

Peace
- Ask God to remind you of times that you caused peace yesterday. Celebrate this and agree with God about it.

Patience
- Ask God to remind you of times that you were patient yesterday. Celebrate this and agree with God about it.

Kindness
- Ask God to remind you of times that you were kind yesterday. Celebrate this and agree with God about it.

Goodness
- Ask God to remind you of times that you truly benefitted someone yesterday. Celebrate this and agree with God about it.

Meekness
- Ask God to remind you of times that you were flexible instead of getting angry yesterday. Celebrate this and agree with God about it.

Faithfulness
- Ask God to remind you of times that you were faithful and persistent yesterday. Celebrate this and agree with God about it.

Self-Control
- Ask God to remind you of times that you moderated what you wanted to do yesterday. Celebrate this and agree with God about it.

Day 32: Qualified, Quality, Quarrel, Quench, Quest, Question, Quit

Qualified

The qualification for getting into heaven and pleasing God is faith. The righteous shall live by faith. God is asking everyone to trust Him -- first in the death of His Son for their sins and then for the specific ways to live a Christian life.

- If you have never asked Jesus to be your Lord and Savior, ask Him now.

Dear Lord,

I ask you to forgive me of my sins and selfishness. I realize that, Jesus, you paid my penalty. I submit to Christ for how I will live my life. Thank you for dying on the cross for my sins.

- If you are a Christian and qualified by the blood of Christ for heaven then be holy in all your behavior.

Quality

- Pray that you would exhibit the qualities of the Beatitudes.
- Pray them as goals that you are affirming:
  - I am humble, teachable, and adaptive.
  - I do grieve my sin, wounds, losses, and pain.
  - I am flexible and calm, making thoughtful requests and wise adaptations.
  - I do pursue the right action, regardless the cost.
  - I am merciful.
  - I do fill my mind with pure thoughts and images.
  - I create harmony between myself and others.
  - I am willing to be insulted and hated for Christ and what is right.

Quarrel
- Pray that you would not quarrel with people needlessly.
- Pray that God would show you how to make up with anyone you may be quarreling with or have been quarreling with.

Quench
- Pray that you will not quench the Spirit of God.
- Pray that you will be alert to the promptings of the Holy Spirit.

Quest
The Scriptures say that our life will be filled with opportunities to do good works that have been planned for us from before the world began (*Ephesians 2:10)*. This then is the quest for each of us – finding and doing the good works that we have been assigned.
- Pray that God would show you each day, each week, each month, and each year what great things you can do. Then do them.

Question
What are the five key questions you would like to ask God?
1.
2.
3.
4.
5.

Quit
- Ask God for the energy to not quit.
- Ask God to send you the people and the resources to not give in to unrighteousness.

Day 33: Rapid, Rapture, Real, Reap, Receive, Recognition

Rapid

Rapid prayers are prayers that are quick sentence requests.

- What are five quick things you are dealing with now that you want God to know about and help you with?

1.
2.
3.
4.
5.

Rapture

One day the trumpet will sound and Christ will return. It may be today.

- Pray that you are ready today to be caught up in the air to be with Christ.
- Ask God to show you what you need to do to be ready for Him to return today. What you need to start. What you need to stop!!
- Pray that God would return today and begin the righteousness of Christ.

Real

- Ask God to show you how to listen to yourself.
- Ask God to allow you to be real and authentic in your relationships.
- Ask God to energize you toward your hidden righteous goals.

Reap

The Bible says that whatever we sow, that is what we are going to reap.

- Ask God to show you the choices that you made in the past that resulted in your present.
- Ask God to show you what decisions you are making right now and the crops that they will grow.
- Ask God to show you the choices you can make that will grow into a great life that is glorifying to God.

Receive

The Scriptures remind us, "What do you have that you have not received?" "If you have received it, why do you boast as though you have not received it?"

Since it is true that we have received everything, it is very helpful at times to acknowledge that we have received it. He has provided so much, and at times He allows you to cooperate with Him to increase the blessings of the opportunities He sends, but they are still gifts from Him.

- Tell God that you realize that everything in your home you have received from Him.
- Tell God that all your abilities, gifts, and talents have been received from Him.
- Tell God that you realize that all your relationships are gifts from Him.
- Tell God that your work and your successes are received from Him.
- Tell God that you are thankful for all the good things about your church.

Recognition

Everyone has people in their life who make their life and work possible. These people need to be recognized for all they do.

- Ask God who you should recognize this week for their contribution to your life.

133

- Ask God how you should recognize them.

Reconcile

God clearly wants us to live at peace with others if at all possible. This means that we need to reconcile with those who we have offended or who have offended us.

- Ask God to help you see who you need to reconcile with so that the cause of Christ and your health and welfare would improve.
- Ask God to show you how to reconcile with these people.

Day 34: Schemes of Satan

In 2 Corinthians 2:10,11, the apostle Paul tells the Corinthians to forgive a lapsed brother because otherwise it would be easy to fall into a scheme of Satan. What are the schemes of Satan? God has told us all of the ways that the Devil tries to mess up our lives. He has given them to us in the names and titles that the Scriptures give to the being Lucifer.

- Ask God to make you alert to the schemes of Satan that the he is using on you right now and how to combat them. How is he trying to attack you? What schemes is He using on you? Go through each one and see if He is working on you.

Lucifer: Isaiah 14:12 He will entice you to ignore truth, relationships, and ethics to gain the beautiful or the brilliant.

Satan: Job 1 He will oppose you, block you, and become your Adversary.

The Devil: 1 Peter 5:8 He accuses and slanders you to others, yourself, and God.

Tempter: Matthew 4:3 He entices and distracts you away from God's best.

Roaring Lion: 1 Peter 5:8 He wants to scare, intimidate, and bring fear.

Belial: 2 Corinthians 6:15 He wants you to spend time doing worthless things.

Deceiver: Revelation 12:9 He is the master at deception and manipulation.

Father of Lies: John 8   He lies; makes false promises.

Murderer: John 8:44   He uses violence, threat, and hatred to get his way.

Sinner: 1 John 3:8   He wants you to break God's laws.

Beelzebub: Matthew 12:24   He wants you to enjoy dirty actions, habits, and lifestyle.

Enemy: Matthew 13:39   He opposes your righteous ideas and actions.

Evil One: Matthew 13:39   He loves the wicked, perverse, and vile.

Angel of Light: 2 Corinthians 11:13   He appears as a supernatural messenger giving anti-biblical ideas and advice.

God of the World: 2 Corinthians 4:4   He wants you to value and seek after the wrong actions, words, habits, and lifestyles.

The Dragon: Revelation 13   He tries to terrify and intimidate you.

The Snake: Genesis 3   He indirectly wants to influence you away from God's best.

Prince of the Power of the Air: Ephesians 2   He uses demons to tempt, obstruct, warn, and distract you.

Ruler of this World: John 17 He can and does use governments and nations to persecute Christians.

The Wicked One: Matthew 13:19; Ephesians 6:16   He wants you to live outside of God's moral standards and think it is a good thing.

Day 35: Tomorrow, Tactful, Tame, Tarnish, Taste, Teach

Tomorrow

Ask God to give you a glimpse of your full righteous Christian potential five – ten years from now.

- If I am fully living for God and using all that He has given me, in five to ten years show me a glimpse of what each relationship looks like so that I might aim to glorify you maximally in those ways.

I have this kind of relationship with God...

I have this kind of relationship with myself...

I have this kind of relationship with my spouse...

I have this kind of relationship with my family...

I have this kind of relationship with my work...

I have this kind of relationship with my church...

I have this kind of relationship with my finances and possessions...

I have this kind of relationship with my friends...

I have this kind of relationship with my community and country...

I have this kind of relationship with my enemies...

- Ask God specifically for what you have written down.

Tactful

The Bible says that we should wrap the truth in love and not just bludgeon people to death with the truth.

- Ask God to give you the courage to speak the truth tactfully.
- Ask God to give you new ways of being tactful.

Tame

The Scriptures tell us that the most difficult thing to tame is the tongue.

- Ask God to keep you from saying things that would be hurtful to others.
- Ask God to encourage you to speak the entire positive you know about others.
- Ask God to dampen your desire to talk about yourself and your interests.
- Ask God to give you questions to ask others about themselves and their interests.

Tarnish

The Scriptures tell us that we should glorify God with all we do and say.

- Ask God to show you anything that you are currently doing that is tarnishing His reputation by your continued participation in it.
- Ask God to show you the appropriate way to stop doing it.

Taste

The Bible says that we should taste and see that the Lord is good.

- Ask God to show you new ways to taste of His ways and His person.

Teach

God is always trying to teach us and help us grow in the grace and knowledge of the Lord Jesus Christ.

- Ask God to help you see what He is trying to teach you.
- Ask God what you can do to learn it more quickly and deeply.

Day 36: Ultimate, Umpire, Unaccountable, Unafraid, Unbelief

Ultimate

God is the ultimate and is described as All-powerful, All-knowing, Everywhere present, Unchanging, and Transcendent.

- Spend time praising and thanking God that He is all these things -- the ultimate beyond anything that we can ask, think, contemplate, or comprehend.

Umpire

The Scriptures tell us that Jesus will ultimately be the umpire over everyone's life. He will make decisions from His position as God -- knowing our thoughts, actions, and motives. It is said that when Jesus was being crucified on the cross and insulted, He kept entrusting Himself to the God who judges righteously. He did not need to fight back and prove the accusations were not true; He knew that God the Father was His umpire and would decide who was right and who was wrong. Even though He was treated cruelly here, He was rewarded immensely in heaven for doing what was right in spite of the insults, beatings, misunderstandings, and pain.

It is possible that you are involved with situations, circumstances, and people that are not right and you are not in a position to do anything about it. If you can make it right, then do that. But if you cannot, then it is time to hand over to Jesus all vengeance, all hatred, all scheming, and all decisions about who is right and who is wrong.

- Tell God that you are asking Him to be the umpire in your dispute. You are trusting Him to show who is right and who is wrong. You are leaving all vengeance with Him and asking Him to handle all the punishments and rewards.

141

Unaccountable

Many of the problems in our lives arise because we believe that we are not accountable to anyone.

* Ask God to bring into your life, loving and strong accountability partners who will encourage you to do right and discourage you from doing wrong.
* Ask God to show you how to help these people hold you accountable for godly action.

Unafraid

The Scriptures tell us that God loves us and wants to drive fear from our life through His love.

* Tell God what your fears are and ask Him how His love can overcome that particular fear.
* Ask God to show you how to embrace His love in this new way.

Unbelief

The Scriptures talk about two kinds of unbelief. One kind is unbelief that refuses to trust God for a particular action or mission that He is prompting you to do. The second kind of unbelief is a rejection of the truth of the Christian world view. The Devil is constantly attacking us. He wants to have us embrace both kinds of unbelief.

* Ask God to strengthen you against both forms of unbelief.
* Ask God to show you how the Devil is working to undermine your faith.
* Ask God to keep you from ever rejecting the truth of the Christian world view.
* Ask God to empower you so you do not rebel against trusting Him.

Day 37: Vain, Valuable, Victim, Vent, VIP

Vain

The book of Ecclesiastes tells us that life is vain without God, and it is filled with activities and people who will waste our time. If we are not careful, we will allow our lives to go rushing by accomplishing nothing for the Lord but filled with useless activities, interests, and people. It is not wrong to have hobbies and fun interests, but we must make sure that we are not busy accomplishing nothing.

- Ask God to show you the areas where your life has picked up too many empty pursuits.
- Ask God to show what to substitute in the place of the vain things.

Valuable

The Bible states that God will evaluate our life one day, looking for those activities, relationships, accomplishments, and interests that were gold, silver, and precious stones in their quality and ability to glorify God.

- Ask God to show you the activities, relationships, accomplishments, and interests that will glorify Him.
- Ask God to show you how to maximize your value to God and those around you.

Victim

Our culture wants everyone to wallow in how they are the victim because of the things that have happened to them in life. Yet God wants us to be victors through Christ and His love for us.

- Ask God to show you how you can live in the victory of Christ and reject the victim mindset.
- Ask God to show you how to participate in how He is causing everything to work together for God in your life.

Vent

All of us need to vent at times. Even Jesus in the garden needed to vent with the Father as He cried out, "If there is some other way, let this cup pass from me." One of the best places to vent is with God who already knows everything you are feeling and thinking.

- Take a walk, get in your car, or find a secluded spot where you can speak to God about all the things that you are feeling in your life. Talk out loud and tell Him exactly how you feel and what you are thinking.

VIP

God says that He sent His only begotten Son to the earth to live and die for you so that you would have a way to have a relationship with Him. That makes you a VIP.

- Tell God that you are very grateful that He sees you as a Very Important Person.
- Thank God that He was willing to invest so much in you.
- As an acknowledgement of your value to God, say out loud, "I am a very important person to God."

Day 38: Wisdom, Wail, Wave, Walk, Wander, Want, Warfare, Waste

Wisdom

The Scriptures tell us that we should strive after wisdom; that we will find God's direction for our lives. Wisdom is the choice that is the Triple-Win choice: God wins, others win, and you win.

* Pray for God's wisdom so you will see and choose the Triple-Win choice.
* Pray that God would develop the positive aspects of wisdom in your life.
* Pray that God would give you discernment to avoid the foolish tendencies in life.
* Pray that you would respond wisely to the people who are fools in your life.

Wail

There are appropriate times to wail in prayer. To wail is to have deep sorrow and even raised voices at the problems and difficulty. The prophets wailed when their country turned away from the law and precepts of God. Jesus wailed at the tomb of Lazarus and when His own people did not recognize who He was. It is right to wail at injustice.

* Wail with God at the areas where your country is turning from His laws and His precepts. Be specific and let your heart emote at the tragedy that is happening and will happen.
* Wail over those who have been given a clear presentation of Christ and yet turn away from Him and go their own independent way.
* Wail at the injustice that takes place in your society.

Wave

It is appropriate to raise your hands in praise and prayer to the Lord. In 1 Timothy, God tells us to raise holy hands in prayer to the Lord.

- Raise your hands high above your head and praise God for who He is and what He has done for you.
- Raise your hands above your head and ask God to bless you so you can live a more righteous life.

Walk

The Scriptures tell us that if we walk by the Spirit, we will not carry out the desires of the flesh.

- Pray that you would be sensitive and alert to the promptings of the Spirit as to where He wants you to go and what He wants you to do so that you would not give into temptation to just live by the flesh.
- When you are being tempted to be sensual, angry, slanderous, petty, or any other fleshly sins, get real quiet in your soul and listen to the promptings of the Spirit and then do what He says.

Wander

A very famous hymn lyric states that we are, "Prone to wander, Lord, I feel it. Prone to leave the God, I love." Our flesh, the world system, and the Devil will use everything in their power to get us to wander from the will of God. Do not let them.

- Pray that God would show you how you are being tempted to wander from the Lord.
- Pray that you would take advantage of God's grace to turn away from the wandering paths.
- Pray for clarity about God's will today and then do it. If you do the will of the Lord for that day then you will not be wandering. Do not focus on the wandering paths but on the will of God.

Want

The Psalmist David in the famous 23rd Psalm states that the Lord is our shepherd; we shall not want. This means that if God is the one guiding us, we will not have a need that He doesn't supply. Therefore if we are in want, it means one of three things: first, that God's provision is on its way; second, that God has not been our shepherd in some area; and/ or third, we have squandered what He has given us.

- Ask God to be your shepherd in every area of your life.
- Thank God that He will supply your needs.
- Ask God to help you see how He is meeting the needs that you have.

Warfare

The Christian is in a battle with three different enemies that seek to rob them of the joy and power of the Christian life. These three enemies are the world, the flesh, and the Devil. They all conspire to keep you from living out the will of God. What is the will of God? It is summed up in the first and second great commandments. Thou shalt love the Lord your God with all your heart, soul, mind and strength and your neighbor as yourself.

- Ask God to show you how the world, flesh, or Devil is trying to keep you from loving Him, others, and/or yourself.
- Ask God to show you what He wants you to do to love Him, others, and yourself.

Waste

In Jeremiah 15, God tells Jeremiah that there is great reward in taking the wasted times in his life and turning them into positive times of prayer, reflection, and biblical meditation.

- Ask God to show you at least one period of time that is being wasted that could be used for prayer, reflection, and/ or biblical meditation.

147

- Ask God to show you the best way to use this former wasted time.

Day 39: X-Cross, X-Cross, X-Cross

X – Cross

The whole of Christianity is built on the fact that Jesus the God-man lived a perfect human life and voluntarily gave up His sinless life to be crucified on a cross so that as many as received Him could become children of God.

- Thank Christ for His sacrifice and willingness to put up with the shame and torment of the cross so that you would have the opportunity to be in relationship with God.

X – Cross

Like our Lord and Savior, there is a cross waiting for each Christian. The Christian must take up his/her own individual cross and die to self to fulfill the larger purpose of God.

- Ask God to give you courage and love so that you would be willing to die to your selfish desires so that others might be loved and benefitted.
- Ask God to make it clear when you need to die to self and live to the larger purpose of Christ.

X – Cross

Just like our Savior who was laid in a tomb after His death on the cross for our sins and was dead to the impulses of His flesh, we are to die to the fleshly impulses that used to rule our lives. We have died and our life is hidden with Christ in God. We died to the sensual, proud, angry, slanderous, and immoral promptings of the past; and we listen hard to the life-giving promptings and direction of God the Holy Spirit.

- Pray that when the fleshly impulse comes, you will be able to play dead to those impulses and respond to the impulses of God to do the righteous and loving thing.
- Ask God to help you hear His voice clearly.

149

Day 40: Yawn, Yearn, Yesterday, Yield, Yoke

Yawn

The Bible tells us that we are to be alert to the spiritual times in which we live. We are to stay alert in prayer and alert in looking for the Lord's return and alert to the schemes of the Devil.

* Pray that you would not be lulled into complacency.
* Pray that you would be alert to the smallest negative changes and do what you can to correct them.
* Pray that you would be alert to what the Devil is trying to do to tempt you out of the will of God.
* Pray that you would be ready for the return of the Lord.

Yearn

The Scriptures talk about a yearning for the Lord; a desire to be with God and to know Him.

* Pray that you would be filled with a yearning for Him.
* Ask God to give you more of Himself.

Yesterday

God tells us to forget the past and press on towards the high calling of God in Christ Jesus.

* Tell God that you are done with trying to fix the past and you want to move on to building a great future.
* Ask God to show you the direction that your future needs to go.
* Ask God to make you alert to the opportunities that He is already supplying to develop a great future.

Yield

We all have our plans and our ideas and those don't always work out. We must yield to what God is doing and not spend lots of time fighting for our ideas or goals that no longer make sense.

Too many people waste the present and future being bitter about yesterday.

- Yield to God's will in your life, especially if that is different from what you always wanted.
- Yield to what God wants you to do today, especially if it is difficult or distasteful.
- Let God know that you will stop fighting Him when He wants to direct you – He just has to make it clear.

Yoke

Jesus says that living life His way is like being hitched to a new yoke with a new team and a new goal. Jesus wants to teach us how to fill our life with love and make it overflow. His way of living is different and the goal is different. It is not about striving for prestige, power, and money; it is about learning to fill every relationship with love.

- Pray that you will accept this new yoke – this new goal and way of life -- and not rebel.
- Ask God to show you how to love in each area of your life.
- Ask God to forgive you when you rebel and try and live the old way, seeking prestige, power, and money.
- Ask God to give you patience as you wait for the rewards of this new lifestyle.

Day 41: Zeal, Zion, Zero, Zenith, Zone

Zeal

Jesus says after He cleansed the temple of the money changers that "Zeal for the Lord had consumed Him." We all need to be zealous for the Lord.

- Ask God to reignite your passion for the Lord and let it burn brightly.
- Ask God to show you what direction your zeal for the Lord needs to move.
- Pray that you do not become complacent and comfortable in your Christianity while living in a broken and sinful world.

Zion

God has invested a lot of time and love in the Jewish people. He asks us to pray for the peace of Jerusalem.

- Pray for the peace of Jerusalem.
- Pray that the Jewish nation would recognize their Messiah – Jesus of Nazareth.
- Pray that Jesus would return and show the world that He is the Messiah.

Zero

Jesus will judge mankind at the end of history and each individual life.

- Pray that each day of your life would not be a zero in Jesus' estimate but instead be a plus day; a day that He is pleased with you because you trusted Him and relied upon His grace to accomplish His will for that day.
- Pray for those who are right now living for themselves and scoring zero after zero after zero in their eternal scorecard.
- Pray that they would see their need for the Savior and come to faith in Him.

Zenith

The utmost and supreme of everything is God.

- Praise Him that He is the definition of supreme and almighty.
- Praise Him that He is holy above, before, and over every other creature and He is without sin.
- Praise Him that He is the definition of good: beneficial, merciful, loving, gracious, and kind.
- Praise Him that He is the creator and inventor of our universe and all that it contains.

Zone

We all have zones that increase our production, zones that increase our love for God, and zones that tempt us to sin. Sometimes these zones are places, sometimes these zones are times, sometimes these zones involve certain people, and sometimes these zones involve certain things.

- Pray that you would find your productive zones and stay in those zones.
- Pray that you would understand your temptation zones and stay out of those zones.
- Ask God to keep you from your bad zones.
- Pray that God would give you the courage of what you know to be true about yourself so that no matter what others say, you will be in the good zones and stay out of the bad zones.

Prayers:

Answers:

Conclusion

Congratulations you have completed a long period of prayer and are richer and wiser for the experience. What was it like to be able to pray for forty straight days with something new to pray every day? Most likely you found a whole new world of communication with God opened up. Our relationship with God can be improved with increased communication. He has already done all that was needed for a relationship to be possible.

Prayer is a wonderful journey into a relationship with God. I find most Christians would love to go deep with God; they just don't know how to do it. Now you have in your hand a tool for going deep with God: forty days of in-depth prayer prompts. Keep going and repeat the prayers that were helpful the last time. Embrace the wonder of talking with God about everything. Get His insights, ask for His help, and let Him fill you with energy and grace.

The Christian life is a life lived with God at His direction. Do not settle for a half-Christian life which only involves doing your best to follow God's instructions. Take the journey of life with God constantly interacting and learning from Him. Prayer is crucial part of this process.

Please use this prayer guide over and over again. Share it with your friends and take them through this initial process of deep prayer. Ask your small group at church to go through this prayer journey together and see all the discussion and depth it fosters.

Small Group Materials

There are six to eight weeks to this small group. This small group is designed as an active small group. I call them action groups rather than Bible Study because each participant is active, practicing their faith and through that is learning. The members of the small group must participate in the daily activities of prayer and praise or the group will not work out well. This book has two 40-day prayer adventures. Both are forty days or six weeks of daily activities. This small group is designed to stretch your prayer life in new directions and to see answers to prayer that you have never seen before. This group also encourages people to pray together and to talk about the process of experiencing God in their prayer time.

Over the course of the six to eight weeks, the group will put an emphasis on all of the purposes of a dynamic church: Evangelism, Discipleship, Worship, Fellowship, and Compassion. Each week the group will move through four of the five purposes. It is recommended to have a week where the whole group goes together and serves at some kind of service project. Most churches will have a list of recommended compassion and/or service organizations.

Week 1: Introductions and Going Deep in Prayer
Week 2: Going Deep in Prayer
Week 3: Going Deep in Prayer
Week 4: Going Deep in Prayer
Week 5: Going Deep in Prayer
Week 6: Going Deep in Prayer
Week 7: Compassion Project
Week 8: Celebration of the group

Some groups put the Compassion project in week four to make it an integral part of the group life.

157

Week 1

Start the group in prayer.

Introduction
Let everyone introduce themselves.
Tell us your name and anything else about yourself you want us to know.

Evangelism Section: 5 -10 minutes
Ask the members of the group, "Did anyone get a chance to share their faith during this last week?"

If someone did then let that person share.

If no one did then ask the members of the group if they would be willing to pray this prayer, "Dear Lord, I am willing to share my faith this next week. If you want me to share my faith, please have someone come up to me and ask me. If you do not then I do not have to share. In Jesus Christ's name, Amen."

Discipleship Portion: 20-40 minutes
Pass out the books and/or make sure that people already have them.

This book *Going Deep in Prayer: 40 days of In-Depth Prayer* moves the participants through various prayer guides. There is something powerful that takes place when individuals and groups take the time to pray in ways that God has directed us. It is always a stretching and invigorating time.

Prayer is meant to be wonderful conversation between God and the believer. But sometimes sincere believers do not know what to say when they talk to God. This book *Going Deep In Prayer*

158

will help you talk to God about all kinds of different things. Each of the various prayer topics has been chosen for a reason. It will stretch your praying.

Do a brief overview of the various prayer guides and what pages in the book that particular prayer topics begin. Essentially you are giving a tour of the Table of Contents. This will make people feel comfortable with the prayer assignments as they take place. You can ask people to do part one or part two or you can let them choose which they would prefer. Give a sentence or two explaining each of the different prayer guides. Do not try and teach through this material, instead just make sure that people are familiar with these descriptions and their basic meaning.

The Lord's Prayer
The Fruit of the Spirit
Various Forms of Prayer
The Ten Major Relationships
Alphabetic Prayer Guide

The group is an active participatory group. Each day the members of the group will do that day's prayer assignment. They will complete the prayer assignment at some time during the day, making a few notes about what they did and how the time went.

Worship Portion: 10-20 minutes
Ask each person to turn to page 18.
Spend the next 10-20 minutes praising God out loud in the group. This does not have to be loud or emotional, just sincere reflection on the truths about God on page 18. I realize that this may be a little intimidating at first, but it is very easy to tell God that you think it is wonderful that He is a particular way.

People should feel free to jump in and thank God for the elements of His being that strike them. Some groups move through the material in order, giving people time to praise God for an element. Then they move on when everyone seems done with that aspect of God's being. It will be surprising how quickly time goes by once the process gets started.

No one individual should dominate the prayer time, but everyone should get a chance to pray a sentence or two. Keep the prayer time moving by encouraging lots of people to pray. Enjoy the collective praying process.

This first week of praising the Lord in a group breaks that ice about praying out loud in a group. If you have more than 12 people in the group then divide people into groups of three and have the smaller groups be their own prayer circle. The point is to have everyone start praying. If there are too many people in the group, some people will not feel comfortable to pray out loud.

Fellowship Portion: 5-30 minutes
Ask each individual for a prayer request for themselves. This is not a time to ask for other people; the request must be for the individual themselves. Each person is asked to commit to pray at least once during the next week for each person in the group.

If a person does not have a personal prayer request then the members of the group can pray anything they would like for that person. We call these "whatever" prayers. It is always interesting to hear what people prayed when they were released to pray whatever they felt led to pray for that person. It is always interesting to hear what people prayed for and what God answered.

Close in Prayer
Have some refreshments for people to enjoy.

Week 2

Start the group in prayer.

Introduction
Let everyone introduce themselves again or have name tags.
Tell us your name and anything else about yourself you want us to know.

Evangelism Section: 5 -10 minutes
Ask the members of the group, "Did anyone get a chance to share their faith during this last week?"

If someone did then let them share.

If no one did then ask if they would be willing to pray this prayer, "Dear Lord, I am willing to share my faith this next week. If you want me to share my faith, please have someone come up to me and ask me. If you do not then I do not have to share. In Jesus Christ's name, Amen."

Worship Portion: 20-40 minutes
Take the assignment for that day and pray through it as a group. Enjoy the collective praying process.
The members of the small group should pray using specifically that day's assignments but also any of the previous week's assignments that seem appropriate.

Discipleship Portion: 20-40 minutes
It is important to let people talk about what happened when they spent the time each day in prayer. It is very likely that some people will have powerful times of experiencing God, and others might find the prayer times flat and uneventful.

Which of the days were the most meaningful?

What did you do?

What happened when you prayed?

What did you learn about God? About yourself?

What did you sense God was communicating to you?

How has this prayer exercise changed you?

Fellowship Portion: 5-30 minutes

Ask each individual for a prayer request for themselves.
This is not a time to ask for other people; the request must be for the person themselves. Each person is asked to commit to pray at least once during the next week for each person in the group.

If they do not have a personal prayer request then the members of the group can pray anything they would like for that person. We call these "whatever" prayers. It is always interesting to hear what people prayed when they were released to pray whatever they felt led to pray for that person. It is also interesting to hear which prayers God answered in the life of the person. Make sure that you take time to hear how the prayer requests from the last week turned out.

Close in Prayer

Have some kind of refreshment for people to enjoy.

Week 3

Start the group in prayer.

Introduction
Let everyone introduce themselves again or have name tags.
Tell us your name and anything else about yourself you want us to know.
You might ask a question that will allow people to reveal more about themselves; such as, tell us one job you did at some point in your life that you are no longer doing?

Evangelism Section: 5 -10 minutes
Ask the members of the group, "Did anyone get a chance to share their faith during this last week?" If someone did then let them share.

If no one did then ask if they would be willing to pray this prayer, "Dear Lord, I am willing to share my faith this next week. If you want me to share my faith, please have someone come up to me and ask me. If you do not then I do not have to share. In Jesus Christ's name, Amen."

Worship Portion: 20-40 minutes
Take the assignment for that day and pray through it as a group Enjoy the collective praying process.
The members of the small group should pray using specifically that day's assignments but also any of the previous week's assignments that seem appropriate.

Discipleship portion: 20-40 minutes
It is important to let people talk about what happened when they spent the time each day in prayer. It is very likely that people will have powerful times experiencing God.

Which of the days were the most meaningful? Why?

What did you do?

What happened when you prayed?

What did you learn about God? About yourself?

What did you sense God was communicating to you?

How has this prayer exercise changed you?

Fellowship Portion: 5-30 minutes
Ask each individual for a prayer request for themselves.
This is not a time to ask for other people; the request must be for the person themselves. Each person is asked to commit to pray at least once during the next week for each person in the group.

If they do not have a personal prayer request then the members of the group can pray anything they would like for that person. We call these "whatever" prayers. It is always interesting to hear what people prayed when they were released to pray whatever they felt led to pray for that person. It is also interesting to hear which prayers God answered in the life of the person. Make sure that you take time to hear how the prayer requests from the last week turned out.

Close in Prayer
Have some kind of refreshment for people to enjoy.

Week 4

Start the group in prayer.

Introduction
Let everyone introduce the person to their left.
Tell us their name and something about them that not many people know.

Evangelism Section: 5 -10 minutes
Ask the members of the group, "Did anyone get a chance to share their faith during this last week?" If someone did then let them share.

If no one did then ask if they would be willing to pray this prayer, "Dear Lord, I am willing to share my faith this next week. If you want me to share my faith, please have someone come up to me and ask me. If you do not then I do not have to share. In Jesus Christ's name, Amen."

Worship Portion: 20-40 minutes
Take the assignment for that day and pray through it as a group

Enjoy the collective praying process.

The members of the small group should pray using specifically that day's assignments but also any of the previous week's assignments that seem appropriate.

Discipleship Portion: 20-40 minutes
It is important to let people talk about what happened when they spent the time each day in prayer. It is very likely that people will have powerful times experiencing God.

Which of the days were the most meaningful? Why?

What did you do?

What happened when you prayed?

What did you learn about God? About yourself?

What did you sense God was communicating to you?

How has this prayer exercise changed you?

Fellowship Portion: 5-30 minutes
Ask each individual for a prayer request for themselves.
This is not a time to ask for other people, the request must be for the person themselves. Each person is asked to commit to pray at least once during the next week for each person in the group.

If they do not have a personal prayer request then the members of the group can pray anything they would like for that person. We call these "whatever" prayers. It is always interesting to hear what people prayed when they were released to pray whatever they felt led to pray for that person. It is also interesting to hear which prayers God answered in the life of the person. Make sure that you take time to hear how the prayer requests from the last week turned out.

Close in Prayer
Have some kind of refreshment for people to enjoy.

Week 5

Start the group in prayer.

Introduction
Let everyone introduce someone else in the group.
Tell us their name and something else we did not know.

Evangelism Section: 5 -10 minutes
Ask the members of the group, "Did anyone get a chance to share their faith during this last week?" If someone did then let them share.

If no one did then ask if they would be willing to pray this prayer, "Dear Lord, I am willing to share my faith this next week. If you want me to share my faith, please have someone come up to me and ask me. If you do not then I do not have to share. In Jesus Christ's name, Amen."

Worship Portion: 20-40 minutes
Take the assignment for that day and pray through it as a group

Enjoy the collective praying process.

The members of the small group should pray using specifically that day's assignments but also any of the previous week's assignments that seem appropriate.

Discipleship Portion: 20-40 minutes
It is important to let people talk about what happened when they spent the time each day in prayer. It is very likely that some people will have powerful times of experiencing God. And others might find the prayer times flat and uneventful.

Which of the days were the most meaningful? Why?

What did you do?

What happened when you prayed?

What did you learn about God? About yourself?

What did you sense God was communicating to you?

How has this prayer exercise changed you?

Fellowship Portion: 5-30 minutes

Ask each individual for a prayer request for themselves.
This is not a time to ask for other people, the request must be for the person themselves. Each person is asked to commit to pray at least once during the next week for each person in the group.

If they do not have a personal prayer request then the members of the group can pray anything they would like for that person. We call these "whatever" prayers. It is always interesting to hear what people prayed when they were released to pray whatever they felt led to pray for that person. It is also interesting to hear which prayers God answered in the life of the person. Make sure that you take time to hear how the prayer requests from the last week turned out.

Close in Prayer

Have some kind of refreshment for people to enjoy.

Week 6

Start the group in prayer.

Introduction
Let everyone introduce God to the group and tell the most intense and amazing things about God that has struck them over these last six weeks.

Evangelism Section: 5 -10 minutes
Ask the members of the group, "Did anyone get a chance to share their faith during this last week?" If someone did then let them share.

If no one did then ask if they would be willing to pray this prayer, "Dear Lord, I am willing to share my faith this next week. If you want me to share my faith, please have someone come up to me and ask me. If you do not then I do not have to share. In Jesus Christ's name, Amen."

Worship Portion: 20-40 minutes
Take the assignment for that day and pray through it as a group

Enjoy the collective praying process.

The members of the small group should pray using specifically that day's assignments but also any of the previous week's assignments that seem appropriate.

Discipleship Portion: 20-40 minutes
It is important to let people talk about what happened when they spent the time each day in prayer. It is very likely that some people will have powerful times of experiencing God. And others might find the prayer times flat and uneventful.

Which of the days were the most meaningful? Why?

What did you do?

What happened when you prayed?

What did you learn about God? About yourself?

What did you sense God was communicating to

you? How has this prayer exercise changed you?

Fellowship Portion: 5-30 minutes
Ask each individual for a prayer request for themselves.
This is not a time to ask for other people, the request must be for the person themselves. Each person is asked to commit to pray at least once during the next week for each person in the group.

If they do not have a personal prayer request then the members of the group can pray anything they would like for that person. We call these "whatever" prayers. It is always interesting to hear what people prayed when they were released to pray whatever they felt led to pray for that person. It is also interesting to hear which prayers God answered in the life of the person. Make sure that you take time to hear how the prayer requests from the last week turned out.

Close in Prayer
Have some kind of refreshment for people to enjoy.

Compassion Week / Farewell Week
As a group do a compassion project together.

Preaching Materials

This material can be a part of a sermon series in which the pastor explores prayer. The following are ideas for various sermon series to preach through a topic like this.

The following are six different approaches to tie this individual and small group material to the preaching of this material.

1. Pick six or seven specific verses and preach those. One each week.

2. Take each of the elements in the Lord's Prayer and preach a sermon on one of them.

3. Take the six different prayer guides and develop each one of these in a sermon, with two weeks being used to develop the various kinds of prayer.

4. Take six or seven different narrative passages where the main person prays and teach prayer in this way. Examples: Moses, Hannah, David, Samuel, Hezekiah, Jesus, Peter, Paul, etc.

5. Spend six or seven weeks in one passage such as the Lord's Prayer. Luke 18; Ephesians 1:18-2:1

6. Preach the topic that is discussed on the particular day in the book that your people will be going through that Sunday.

7. Preach one sermon about prayer at the beginning of the series to launch the series and then let the small groups cover the rest of the material.

171

About The Author

Gil Stieglitz is an internationally recognized author, speaker, catalyst, counselor, professor, and leadership consultant. He is Executive Pastor of Adventure Christian Church, a mega-church of 4,000 in Roseville, California. He teaches at Christian Universities and graduate schools in practical theology (Biola, William Jessup, Western Seminary). He is the President of Principles to Live By, an organization committed to teaching God's principles in a life-giving way. He sits on the board of Courage Worldwide, an organization that builds homes throughout the world to rescue children forced into sexual slavery. He has been a denominational executive for fifteen years with the Evangelical Free Church of America and was the senior pastor of a vibrant church in southern California for seventeen years.

Other Resources by Gil Stieglitz

BOOKS

Becoming Courageous

Breaking Satanic Bondage

Deep Happiness: The 8 Secrets

Delighting in God

Developing a Christian Worldview

God's Radical Plan for Husbands

God's Radical Plan for Wives

Going Deep In Prayer: 40 Days of In-Depth Prayer

Leading a Thriving Ministry

Marital Intelligence

Mission Possible: Winning the Battle Over Temptation

Secrets of God's Armor

Spiritual Disciplines of a C.H.R.I.S.T.I.A.N

They Laughed When I Wrote Another Book About
    Prayer, Then They Read It

Touching the Face of God: 40 Days of Adoring God

Why There Has to Be a Hell

If you would be interested in having Gil Stieglitz
speak to your group, you can contact him
through the website
www.ptlb.com

PODCASTS
Becoming A Godly Parent
Biblical Meditation: The Keys of Transformation
Deep Happiness: The 8 Secrets
Everyday Spiritual Warfare Series
God's Guide to Handling Money
Intensive Spiritual Warfare Series
Spiritual War Surrounding Money
The 4 Keys To A Great Family
The Ten Commandments
Thrive Conference:

> Marital Intelligence: There are only 5 Problems in Marriage
> Raising your Leadership Level: Double Your Impact
> Spiritual Warfare: Using the Weapons of God to Win Spiritual Battles

If you would be interested in having Gil Stieglitz
speak to your group, you can contact him
through the website
www.ptlb.com

CPSIA information can be obtained
at www.ICGtesting.com
Printed in the USA
FSOW01n0641200515
7277FS